MYSTERIOUS GEORGIA

MYSTERIOUS GEORGIA

SHERMAN CARMICHAEL

Illustrations by Jason McLean

THE
History
PRESS

Published by The History Press
Charleston, SC
www.historypress.com

First published 2021

Manufactured in the United States

ISBN 9781467149266

Library of Congress Control Number: 2021938537

Notice: The information in this book is true and complete to the best of our knowledge. It is offered without guarantee on the part of the author or The History Press. The author and The History Press disclaim all liability in connection with the use of this book.

To Beverly Carmichael for her many hours of correcting my mistakes, Ric Carmichael, Tamara Carmichael, Blake Mahaffey, Sean Mahaffey, my attorney Gregg Askins, Lynette Goodwin and Cindy James.

CONTENTS

CONTENTS

CONTENTS

JUST A THOUGHT

Georgia's claim to fame as one of the South's most haunted states includes stories of ghosts from every period since the settlement of Georgia. The Revolutionary War and the Civil War brought more ghost stories. These stories include haunted houses, churches, graveyards, police departments, fire departments, lighthouses, bridges, tunnels, hotels, military bases and many more.

Why do these restless spirits remain here on earth and not move on? Can they stay at their will, or does some other force keep them here, keeping them from moving on? Do they have unfinished business? Perhaps they didn't have time to say goodbye to a loved one, or they were not ready to go. There are many reasons we can speculate on, but it's all just theory.

There are many theories about what a ghost is and why it stays here. Let's examine a few. Could it be that an event in history was caught in time and destined to be replayed over and over for eternity and if you are at the right place at the right time you can get a glimpse of it? How do ghosts remain dressed in the clothes that they were killed in if they are the spirits of humans?

For something whose very existence is yet to be scientifically proven, there are a lot of people who seriously believe in ghosts. There are a lot of people who like to believe that expensive ghost hunting toys are the answer to a problem that has plagued mankind since the beginning. I have yet to see one that the so-called results can be proven.

However, UFOs have been seen since the beginning of recorded history. Incidents are even recorded in the Bible.

> *The Second Book of Kings 2:11*
> *Then it happened, as they continued on and talked that suddenly a chariot of fire appeared with horses of fire, and separated the two of them; and Elijah went up by a whirlwind into heaven.*

> *Ezekiel 1:4*
> *Then I looked and behold a whirlwind was coming out of the north, a great cloud with raging fire engulfing itself; and the brightness was all around it and radiating out of its midst like the color of amber, out of the midst of the fire. Also from within it came the likeness of four living creatures, and this was their appearance; they had the likeness of man. Each one had four faces, and each one had four wings. Their legs were straight, and the soles of their feet were like the soles of calves' feet. They sparkled like the color of burnished bronze.*

UFOs still show up on a regular basis. From law enforcement officers, military personnel, astronauts and sailors to even Jimmy Carter, people from around the world have seen something they could not identify in the sky. Some have seen them land, while others have reported being abducted by aliens. There have been a number of reported UFO crashes covered up by the government.

I keep telling myself that I can't expect people to share my interests in ghosts, UFOs and other strange and mystifying things. Yet when I do a book signing or a talk, I find new people who want to share their experiences with me. When I ask them for an interview for an upcoming book, they are glad to give it but without the use of their name. People are afraid of public ridicule, problems at work or with their family. When are people going to face the fact that there are things out there that we don't understand? There could be a simple answer to it that we haven't discovered yet.

What did humans think when they saw the first comet or meteor shower?

Like many who grew up in the South, I've heard ghost stories as far back as I can remember. Many of those were just tall tales, but others were stories of things that actually happened and have been passed down through the years.

Monsters like Bigfoot (United States), the Loch Ness Monster (Scotland), the Lizard Man (South Carolina), the Lake Norman Monster (North Carolina) and Altamaha Ha (Georgia) are found in every state and country in the world.

New incidents happen and new locations are discovered right here in our backyard. Many of the sites in this book are worth a visit. If you want to visit these places and they are on private property, get the owner's permission before going on the property. If the place is open to the public, then follow the rules.

I invite you dear reader to open your mind and look at a world full of seemingly impossible things.

FRANKLIN COUNTY CRYBABY BRIDGE

It seems that about every county in every state has a crybaby bridge, and Franklin County, Georgia, is no different. There are two different stories that go with this bridge. As with many other haunted bridges, the facts are kind of scarce.

The first story is that a lady and her baby were riding in a horse-drawn carriage on their way home. When they got on the bridge, something scared the horse, overturning the carriage and killing the mother and child.

Another story happened in the days before the Civil War when there were a lot of plantations in the area. A plantation owner and a woman he enslaved were engaged in a secret affair. She became pregnant. The plantation owner did not want anyone to know about his extracurricular activity; therefore, he had to hide the evidence. One day shortly after the baby was born, the plantation owner was riding in his horse-drawn wagon and saw the woman and baby crossing the bridge. Seizing his opportunity, he ran the woman and baby off the bridge, killing both of them.

Now for the ritual to summon the ghosts. Park your car on the bridge, turn off the headlights and put the keys on top of the hood and say three times, "Rosemary I have your baby." The woman will appear, and you will hear a baby cry.

Another version of the ritual says to park your car on the bridge, turn off your headlights, put your keys on the hood and then get back in the car. Close the doors and yell, "I killed your baby." The doors of the car will lock by themselves, and the ghost of the mother will appear.

Sometimes you may hear horse's hooves on the bridge. You may also hear a baby crying and see the shadow of a figure that is supposed to be the mother.

EUHARLEE COVERED BRIDGE

Euharlee covered bridge is a lattice-truss design structure. It fastens together with wooden pegs instead of nails. The lattice trusses consist of planks crisscrossing at forty-five to sixty-degree angles. It crosses over the Euharlee Creek in the town of Euharlee, Bartow County, Georgia.

The bridge was built after the raging creek swept away an old bridge on the property of Daniel Lowry. The collapse of the bridge killed one man and his mule. They were drowned in the accident.

The current bridge was built in 1886 by Horace King's son Washington King and Johnathan H. Burke. The bridge spans 138 feet. It was designed by Horace King, but the senior King was too ill to be involved in the actual building of the bridge.

This area may have been settled as early as 1808. In the 1840s, the area grew when a gristmill began operations. The gristmill was powered by the Euharlee Creek. The early settlement was known as Burgess or Burgess Mill. It was incorporated in 1852 as Euharleeville. Residents dropped the "ville" when a new charter was passed in 1870. The mill was sold to Daniel Lowry, who was instrumental in getting the current structure built.

A local legend says that a young Indian girl was abducted shortly after the bridge was built and taken there to be beaten and hanged. People who have had an experience on the bridge say you can hear the sound of the rope creaking under her weight and the sound of her soft cries—that is, if you visit the bridge at the right time.

Another story about a young girl dying on the bridge tells of a small white girl traveling with her daddy by wagon. The young girl was being rambunctious and jumping up and down on the seat of the wagon. As they

were crossing the bridge, she jumped up and caught her long hair in the rafters, and when she came down it broke her neck.

No record of the death of any girl on the Euharlee Bridge could be found.

One lady who was visiting the bridge and taking a picture suddenly fell forward, dropping her camera. She insisted that she had been pushed hard from behind. The problem was there was no one behind her. Some people say they have heard the sound of a girl crying. Others say that they have seen the spirit of an Indian girl hanging from the rafters of the bridge.

The haunting at Euharlee Bridge has been investigated extensively. Of course, there are mixed results. Some say the creaking is a natural sound made by the wooden bridge while others say that when the wind blows, the old wooden bridge creaks and rattles. Others say that the creek can sound like it is singing or crying depending on how fast it's moving.

Traffic was stopped on the Euharlee Covered Bridge in 1980 when a new two-lane bridge was built. The bridge is owned by the county and closed to the public at night.

CONCORD COVERED BRIDGE

This historic covered bridge crosses Nickajack Creek in Smyrna, Cobb County. This historic bridge dates back to 1872. It was added to the National Register of Historic Places in 1980. The one-lane Concord Bridge is 131 feet, 7 inches long and 16 feet wide.

It has the highest traffic count of all covered bridges in the state of Georgia combined; between seven thousand and ten thousand cars cross the bridge each day. In the 1950s, steel beams were added to support the bridge, and additional concrete piers were added. Steel beams were added to protect the bridge from being hit by careless drivers. These beams are hit about once a month, mostly by vehicles that are too high or have a load too high for the bridge.

After receiving about $803,000 worth of repairs, the bridge reopened in mid-December 2017. The bridge is flanked on both sides by multiple warning signs with flashing lights warning drivers of the low clearance. If you plan to ghost hunt at this bridge at night, do not stop on the bridge. There's so much traffic that you're probably going to cause an accident and just might become a ghost yourself.

And now for the ghost stories—as usual there's more than one version of the story and, of course, the ritual.

In 1874, the three-year-old son of John Reed wandered to the Ruff's gristmill and made his way to the upper floor. He got his clothes caught in a piece of revolving machinery. According to the account of the accident

in the *Marietta Daily Journal*, the miller went up to the upper floor and found the child stripped of his clothes, gashed, bleeding and a lifeless wedge in the machinery.

Residents who believe the bridge is haunted think that the young boy could be one of the ghosts haunting the bridge. During the 1800s, several children met their maker near the bridge. One legend says that a group of children drowned beneath the bridge. No details were ever given about this tragedy. There have been various explanations for the deaths, including a bus wreck on the bridge. Another legend tells a couple of young girls who drowned or were drowned in the water below the bridge.

The story goes that if you park your car on the bridge at night, turn off your lights and put some chocolate candy on the roof, you can hear scurrying feet running over your car. When you look, the chocolate candy will be gone and there will be little handprints on your car. Some say you can hear the girls laughing as they climb on top of your car to get the candy. Sometimes you can feel your car being moved as if being pushed. Sometimes you can hear sounds of children speaking or laughing.

CONCORD COVERED BRIDGE HISTORICAL MARKER

The Concord Covered Bridge constructed in the Queenpost design was built in 1872 by Daniell and Ruff, who owned land and mills nearby. It replaced a bridge believed to have been built in the 1840s and destroyed during the Civil War. The Concord Covered Bridge has the distinction of being the only covered bridge still in use on a public highway in the metropolitan Atlanta area. The Girl Scouts of the Nickajack Association placed this marker in 1976 to commemorate the 200th birthday of the United States of America.

STOVALL MILL COVERED BRIDGE

Located in White County near Helen in the lush north Georgia forest is Georgia's smallest short span covered bridge. Three different sources give three different lengths: 33.00 feet, 37.00 feet and 36.87 feet. The Stovall Mill Covered Bridge crosses the Chickamauga Creek in White County. It's well worth taking time out of your busy schedule to visit, and there's a small parking area. Bring the family; it is a lovely place for relaxing and a picnic. However, the bridge has been vandalized by some less-than-desirable people who painted graffiti on the inside.

Fred Dover used to own the land in that area. Dover built a water-powered mill complex that included a shingles mill, a sawmill and a gristmill. He also constructed a milldam on the river. He built the covered bridge to cross over the Chickamauga River. For years, the bridge served as an important link between Cleveland and Clayton Roads before the road was moved. The bridge was washed away in the early 1890s.

In 1895, a new covered bridge was built by Will Pardue to replace the old bridge. In 1917, Fred Stovall bought the water-powered mill complex for which the bridge is now named.

In 1964, the milldam and mill complex were washed away in a flood, but the bridge still remains. The bridge is now a tourist attraction and was used in the movie *I'd Climb the Highest Mountain*, which was filmed in 1951.

As with many old bridges, there's a ghost story or two that go along with the crossing. People say don't cross Stovall Mill Covered Bridge unless you ready to face whatever is calling out after dark. The legend that goes along with the Stovall Mill Covered Bridge says that if you stand on the bridge at night you'll hear a horse-drawn carriage coming across the bridge. Sometimes you might even hear babies crying. The origins of these hauntings are unknown.

GHOSTS OF CAMP CREEK TRAIN WRECK

The train, Southern Engine Number 7, along with two coaches and a Pullman Sleeper car, left Macon, Georgia, at 7:10 p.m. Railroad engineer J.T. Sullivan was at the controls. Sullivan was a substitute engineer on that run. The scheduled engineer's daughter became sick, and the engineer wouldn't leave her.

The train arrived in McDonough, Georgia, on schedule. When another train was going to be late, Sullivan received orders to leave McDonough and head north to Atlanta. At 9:45 p.m., Sullivan pulled Engine Number 7 out, departed McDonough and headed toward Atlanta without its usual load of passengers. Most of the passengers were railroad employees. It was raining hard and had been for three straight weeks. Some of the passengers were a little nervous about traveling in such weather. Sullivan just said, "We'll have breakfast in Atlanta or in hell."

Shortly after leaving McDonough on June 23, 1900, the train was just outside of town when it came up on the Camp Creek Trestle. Sullivan saw the trestle's brick supports had been washed away by the raging waters and applied the brakes, but it was too late. The trestle collapsed under the weight of the train, sending it into the rushing water sixty feet below.

The engine and two coaches burst into flames shortly after piling up in the water. The Pullman car and the ten people on it were the only survivors. Thirty-nine people went to their reward that night in the horrific train accident.

The train was called Old Number 7, not because it was christened that but because it was the engine on route seven between Macon and Atlanta, a stretch of about one hundred miles one way.

Flagman J.J. Quinlan was the first to climb the embankment and saved two women from Boston. Quinlan then ran along the track two miles in the rain, stopping along the way to notify people of the accident and the help needed before he reached the train depot to inform the depot manager about the accident. Quinlan got to the depot in time to stop another train that was coming. The entire population of McDonough was quickly mobilized shortly after Quinlan delivered the news. A train with doctors and ministers arrived the next morning.

As the dead bodies were recovered, they were carted back to McDonough in horse-drawn buggies to the two funeral homes, the B.B. Carmichael and F.F. Bunn and Company. The coffins were laid out on McDonough Square for identification by their families. Some had no identification on them and were burned so badly that they were never identified. The unidentified were laid to rest in unmarked graves in the local cemetery.

What is often called Georgia's own *Titanic* story took place on June 23, 1900. The Camp Creek Train Crash is one of the great tragedies and even greater triumph with the community coming together to help.

Is the weeping woman who has been seen in the Dunn House/Globe Hotel one of the train victims? Ghostly activity has been reported on the McDonough Square. The building that once housed the B.B. Carmichael Funeral Home is now the Season's Bistro. A pair of diners in the restaurant saw a man preparing the body of a woman in the area that is now the women's restroom. One of the diners described the man to the restaurant owner. The restaurant owner was shocked when he realized it was the ghost of B.B. Carmichael. Many places around the square are considered haunted by the ghost of the dead who were laid out in the square.

ST. SIMONS LIGHTHOUSE

The beautiful 104-foot lighthouse on St. Simons Island, Georgia, seems idyllic. The lighthouse was considered to be isolated before being linked to the mainland.

On March 16, 1804, Congress appropriated $7,000 to build a lighthouse on St. Simons Island. In the early 1800s, plantation owner James or John Couper (depending on the source) owned a plantation on the southern end of St. Simons Island. The government needed land to build the lighthouse on, so Couper sold the government four acres of land for $1.

On March 3, 1807, Congress provided $19,000 for the lighthouse project. A notice appeared in the *Savannah Advertiser* looking for a qualified builder to construct an octagonal brick lighthouse. It would be supported by a stone foundation and secured by a substantial door with iron hinges.

James Gould, having newly arrived from England, answered the ad in the newspaper. Gould suggested that the lighthouse be constructed out of tabby. Tabby is a local building material that made from a mixture of lime, water, sand and oyster shells. Gould also suggested other minor changes to the design. The government approved Gould's changes and awarded him the contract.

Gould had a ready-made supply of building materials needed. He would use the ruins of Fort Frederica, which had been built in 1736. Gould completed the seventy-five-foot tower in late 1810 at a cost of $13,775. The oil lamps were suspended on chains to serve as the original light source.

On May 4, James Gould was officially appointed lighthouse keeper by President Madison. Gould was given a salary of $400 a year, and he served as keeper of the lighthouse for twenty-seven years. He was also paid $1,700 to build a keeper's dwelling.

In 1838, it was noticed that the original eight-inch reflectors were too small. In 1847, nine lamps with fourteen-inch reflectors were installed in the lantern room. In 1856, the lights were replaced with a third-order Fresnel lens.

During the Civil War, when Confederate troops left the island in 1862, they dynamited the tower and keeper's house so they wouldn't fall into the Union forces hands. After the Civil War was over, Georgia architect Charles B. Cluskey drew up the plans for a new lighthouse and keeper's house. Congress appropriated $45,000 on March 2, 1867, for a new lighthouse.

In the fall of 1869, the contract was awarded to the lowest bidder with a completion date around June or July 1870. However, difficulties in getting the building material pushed the completion date to November 1, 1870. During the summer, the contractor fell ill and expired. One of the bondsmen stepped up to complete the work, but unfortunately, he also died at the lighthouse.

With the lighthouse standing at only fifty-one feet high, the other bondsman stepped up to finish the lighthouse. A Third Order L. Sautter Fresnel lens was installed, and the lighthouse first cast its light on the island on September 1, 1872. The lens was a fixed lens, but it had four flash panels that revolved and the lens produced a bright flash once every minute.

Bradford B. Brunt was hired as the first keeper of the new lighthouse. Brunt was also given an assistant to help with the work around the lighthouse. Brunt and his assistant repeatedly complained about the unhealthy living conditions on the island. Eventually, the lighthouse board took some action and agreed to drain the ponds in 1875.

On a Sunday morning in March 1880, lighthouse keeper Frederick Osborne and his assistant John Stevens had a duel on the lighthouse grounds. Stevens killed Osborne. The duel was over the fact that one of the men made unwanted advances toward the other man's wife. Stevens was acquitted of the murder charge. That apparently didn't make Osborne happy in the hereafter. Some people say Osborne keeps coming back.

In 1890, a brick oil house was built for storing the kerosene, which replaced the expensive whale oil as the lamp fuel. In 1934, electricity replaced the kerosene. In 1950, the lighthouse was automated.

During Carl Svendsen's service as lighthouse keeper, which lasted from 1907 to 1935, he and his wife kept hearing mysterious footsteps they could not explain. People visiting the lighthouse claim to hear footsteps in the tower when there is no one there to make them. Visitors to the lighthouse have reported hearing footsteps on the staircase and sometimes smell the light keeper's tobacco smoke.

In 1908, the light keeper's wife was having trouble with the light machinery while her husband was away, and she called out to the spirit of Osborne for help. When she turned around to face the machinery, she saw his ghostly figure working on it and fainted. When she awoke, the light was working.

St. Simon Lighthouse is listed in the National Register.

GHOSTS OF TYBEE LIGHTHOUSE

The first Tybee Lighthouse was ordered in 1732 by General James Oglethorpe, governor of the thirteenth colony. Under the direction of Noble Jones of the Wormsloe Plantation, work began on the first day mark (a lighthouse without a light) built on Tybee Island, Georgia. The day mark was completed in 1736.

It was octagonal and built out of bricks and cedar piles. The day mark stood ninety feet tall. The Tybee Island day mark was the tallest structure of its kind in America, but storms and beach erosion took their toll. Five years after the first one's completion, a new day mark was commissioned. Work had begun and was progressing on the new day mark when a storm moved in and swept the old day mark away in August 1741.

In 1742, a second day mark was built by a man named Thomas Sumner. This was the second day mark built on Tybee Island. This one stood ninety-four feet tall with a very tall flagpole. By 1748, the sea had risen to within thirty feet of the day mark. Piles were driven down into the sand to support the foundation. This did not help, so the sea continued until it reached the door. Time was running out for this day mark.

In 1768, the general assembly authorized a new day mark to be built. For this day mark, a site well removed from the encroaching sea was chosen. The new day mark was completed in 1773 by John Mullryne. It was made of sturdy bricks with wooden stairs and landings.

In 1790, the colony of Georgia ratified the Constitution and yielded the day mark to the federal government. The U.S. Lighthouse Establishment took over the operation and turned it into a lighthouse in 1791. The lighthouse was fitted with reflectors and spermaceti candles. It was soon upgraded to oil lamps.

In order to form a navigation range for ships entering the narrow Savannah River, a second tower was added to the site of the completed lighthouse in 1822. In 1857, both towers received Fresnel lenses. During the Civil War Confederate soldiers burned what they could of the lighthouses, but they removed the precious Fresnel lens when they pulled out.

Construction on the fourth of the Tybee Island lighthouses began in 1866 but was delayed due to an outbreak of cholera. When the new lighthouse was finished, it stood on the first sixty feet of the preexisting tower. The finished lighthouse was 154 feet high and equipped with a larger Fresnel lens.

In 1871, the lighthouse was hit by a hurricane. The damage was so serious that the crew decided to replace the wooden parts with iron. Lighthouse keeper's houses were then built on the five-acre property. In 1933, electricity was run to the lighthouse. The staff was reduced to one light keeper. In 1972, the lighthouse became automated.

In 1999, the Tybee Island Historical Society began major restoration work on the lighthouse. In 2002, the National Historic Lighthouse Preservation Act allowed this group of locals and historians to repaint the lighthouse in the 1916–66 black and white.

Today, the Tybee Island lighthouse's original beacon still shines brightly. The Tybee Island lighthouse is open for public tours and is one of the most intact historic lighthouses remaining in America. No lighthouse can be complete without a few ghost stories. Let's take a look at Tybee's.

A staff member claims to have seen an apparition of a man in the first assistant keeper's house. People have reported hearing constant footsteps. People have heard whistling when no one is whistling and witnessed the front door trying to open when no one's there. There have been sightings of a small girl running down the stairs of the lighthouse warning visitors not to go any farther up the staircase. She is dressed in period clothing. The apparition of a man in light keeper's clothes has been seen standing by the lighthouse.

SURRENCY GHOST LIGHT

The Surrency ghost light (called spook light by the locals) is located in the town of Surrency, Georgia. The light appears along the Macon/Brunswick Railroad tracks. The Surrency ghost light is a classic example of the ghost light phenomena. Some of the more famous ghost lights are the Marfa Light in Texas, the Brown Mountain Lights in North Carolina and the Bingham Light in South Carolina, just to name a few.

Surrency, Georgia, was incorporated in 1911, a small town of about three hundred people. The Surrency spook light has been reported since the early 1900s and is still going strong today. The site of the Surrency spook light is centralized along a stretch of the Macon/Brunswick Railroad.

The light itself is described as a bright golden yellow ball about the size of a grapefruit. It appears several hundred yards ahead of you on the railroad tracks and hovers silently before starting to move closer. When it gets to a certain distance, it will disappear, and then it will reappear behind you.

Some theories are ball lightning, car headlight reflections seen through the fog, seismic activity, mirages and the ever-popular swamp gas. Some believe that it's connected to the haunting of the A.P. Surrency home. More about that haunting later. Some theorize that the light is caused by some geological anomaly deep under the town.

Cornell University professor of geology Larry Brown was part of a scientific team that in 1985 discovered what may be an ancient reservoir of water or some other fluid lying nine miles beneath the forest in Surrency.

Professor Brown described the reservoir as about two miles in diameter and shaped like a contact lens. He noted, "We really don't have a good idea what the formation is composed of. If it is water, it would upset a lot of scientific theories as it is theoretically impossible for water or other fluid to exist at such a great depth due to the intense heat and pressure."

SURRENCY HOME POLTERGEIST

This story comes out of Surrency in Appling County and was been witnessed by hundreds. They came from as far away as England and Canada.

Dating back to the 1800s, long before Surrency was a town, it was a farming community. On the edge of the Altamaha River Swamp was a farming family named Surrency. They owned and lived in a large two-story house near the railroad tracks on the outskirts of the community. The Surrency family had eight children ranging in age from three to twenty-one. Although they had a little more wealth than the others in the area, the Surrencys were just your garden-variety normal family. They also owned another farm in another town. Allen Powel Surrency was a sawmill operator and the founder of the small town of Surrency in southeastern Georgia.

When Surrency returned home from a trip to Hazelhurst in October 1872, he was in for a surprise. A short time after his arrival back home, strange things started happening. The Surrencys saw things that would change their lives forever. Glass tumblers slid off the slab, and the crockery fell to the floor and broke. Books started to fall off their shelves. Windows started slamming shut and then flying open. Doors were violently slamming shut without any help. These ghostly happenings were mild compared to what was to come. Tables began flying through the air; mirrors were shattering in the hallways. The clock began to strike thirteen, and the hands would spin wildly backward and forward. Bricks, smoothing irons, tin pans, water buckets and pitchers began to fall in other parts of the house.

Every time the Surrencys ate at the table, the food would end up being thrown in their laps or across the room or on the floor. Eating utensils were bending or twisting while in the hands. The family began losing sleep and not getting enough to eat.

As time went on, the incidents increased. While the two boys were talking to a visiting minister in the parlor, a blazing log flew out of the fireplace and across the room. The minister cut his visit short. Evil red eyes began to appear around the property and around the house at night. Bricks fell out of the sky, and disembodied voices were heard screaming, crying or laughing around the property.

Eventually, the ghost or whatever it was became more violent, targeting the youngest girl in the house. It would lift her out of bed at night, pull her hair at random times and flip the bed over sideways, throwing her to the floor. Hot bricks began falling from nowhere and landing on the roof of the house and in the yard. A pair of boots walked across the floor on their own. Tables would dance around the room. Several hogs and chickens appeared in the living room out of nowhere.

The attacks on their daughter Clementine were the last straw for the Surrency family. They decided it was time for them to pack it up and move. But the ghosts were not going to let that happen without a fight. A fireplace poker lifted out of its resting place, floated down the hall and hit one of the boys on the head several times while the younger boy helplessly watched. The boy was left bleeding on the floor as the poker floated back to its original place.

In an effort to rid the house and family of the ghostly activity, Surrency sought the help of the clergy and scientists as well as spirit mediums and psychics. None succeeded in ridding the house of what had taken up residence in the home. Surrency wrote a letter to the *Savannah Morning News* describing the events that were happening.

There were several theories from the locals. One theory was that Surrency was in league with the devil. Another theory was that the entire Surrency family were psychic people.

These ghostly activities were witnessed by hundreds of people from around the world. The Surrency house had become a tourist attraction. The activities attracted scientists, researchers, spiritualists, mediums and religious officials from all over. The Surrency family finally did move out and left the house abandoned for years. The house ended up burning in 1925. Allen Surrency died in 1877.

This case has all the hallmarks of poltergeist activity. It was one of the most famous hauntings in the history of the South. What made the Surrency haunting so unique is that it was one of the most verified hauntings in American history.

SCREVEN GHOST LIGHT

Screven began as a railroad community around 1847. It wasn't incorporated into a town until 1907. In the late 1800s, the Captain Christopher Columbus Grace family contributed to the town's economic development. The Grace family was instrumental in the local economy into the late 1900s by opening a turpentine operation and running several trade stores. Captain Christopher Columbus Grace was the founding member of the Screven Methodist Episcopal Church.

In 1857, the Savannah, Albany and Gulf Railroad Company's line from Savannah to Screven (then known as Station Seven) was finished when the trestle was built over the Altamaha River at Doctortown. The town was named for Dr. James Procter Screven of the Atlantic and Gulf Railroad. After Screven's death in 1859, his son John Bryan Screven took over the railroad.

The town was originally in the Fourth Land District of Appling County, but the county line was redrawn after the Civil War. The town of Screven was then located in Wayne County, and it was the largest town in the county because of its association with the railroad.

In the early 1900s, Screven officials fought the illegal sale of alcohol. Residents repealed the prohibition on alcohol sales in 1907. Local liquor license fees could be as high as $10,000 as officials tried to curb the sale of alcohol.

In March 2005, Screven was hit by a tornado, devastating the town. No one was killed, but the damage was extensive. People were trapped in their homes and businesses.

Screven is widely known for its ghost light. The light most commonly appears late at night, particularly after rain and following the passing of a train. The light is a glowing white ball that floats and swings back and forth along the railroad tracks. It often flashes bright before dimming. It can disappear and then reappear, flashing.

Of course, there are several theories about what the ghost light is. Scientists have checked out the light with no significant answers. The favorite theory is that it is the spirit of a railroad flagman on the Seaboard Coast Line who was decapitated in an accident between Screven and Jesup. The light is believed to be the lantern the flagman swings while looking for his head.

Late one evening on February 19, 1884, a southbound train on the Savannah, Florida and Western Railroad overshot where it was supposed to stop at Screven Station and collided with a northbound train waiting on a siding. The only injury was Engineer Ford, who got his leg caught between the engine and the tender, crushing it from the knee down to his ankle. Two physicians amputated his leg midway between the thigh and the knee. Engineer Ford died several days later in Waycross on February 21—so much for the headless flagman theory.

Another theory is the ever-popular swamp gas or the lights of Jesup or the lights from nearby cars reflected by atmospheric conditions. The light has been seen for over 125 years at the railroad crossing on Bennett Road. Many natives insist that the light predates the railroad by several decades.

COGDELL GHOST LIGHT

Not much information was available on this ghost light. I did find a few sources on the internet, but the information was limited.

In Clinch County, in the tiny settlement of Cogdell on the edge of the Okefenokee Swamp is a mysterious light known to the locals as the Cogdell spook light. It appears down a deserted dead-end road that paralleled the old train tracks.

If you plan to see the Cogdell light, you'll have to drive down the deserted road, turn off your car and then flash your headlights to summon the light. A greenish yellow glow that seems to come out of the woods will move toward your car—that is, if your visit is timed just right.

Like all ghost lights, there are several different legends that go with the Cogdell ghost light. The first one is that an unknown man was involved in a train accident and his head was removed from his body. The light is supposed to be the unknown man swinging a lantern still looking for his head.

Others believe it's the ghostly glow of a lantern carried by two lovers in an effort to stop a train late at night to get away from their parents. Their parents had forbidden them to see each other. They were tragically killed one night when they were shot by her father, who thought they were prowlers. The ghostly light is a reminder of their love and tragic deaths.

Another legend tied to the Cogdell ghost light is that a train conductor was killed in a train accident and was decapitated. The light is the train conductor still searching for his missing head. Some report that the light will follow your car for a little ways and then disappear abruptly.

Of course, there are several reasonable explanations for the light. It has been explained as swamp gas or hunters with flashlights.

HAUNTED CHETOOGETA MOUNTAIN TUNNEL

The Chetoogeta Mountain Tunnel was started in 1848 and completed two years later. It was used until 1928, when a new and larger tunnel was built close by.

On May 9, 1850, the first Western and Atlantic locomotive passed through the tunnel. The tunnel was 1,477 feet long and 12.5 feet wide. It was a tight squeeze when the first locomotive ran through it in 1850. It was the fastest way to get supplies and people from Atlanta to Chattanooga, even though some trains got stuck in the tunnel and people died. This led to the building of a new parallel tunnel. Irish immigrants were responsible for digging the tunnel.

During the Civil War, whichever side held the tunnel had to guard it against the other side blowing it up. The Chetoogeta Tunnel was the first and oldest railroad tunnel south of the Mason-Dixon line. This subterranean and claustrophobic Civil War attraction has survived over 150 years. It is often referred to as the Tunnel Hill Tunnel.

The State of Georgia tried to entomb it under tons of debris in 1992, but the town of Tunnel Hill rallied to save it. They cleaned out the trash and kudzu vines and eventually opened it to the public. Today, visitors can walk through the tunnel or ride a guided tour through it. The tunnel opened to the public in 2000.

People ask if the tunnel is haunted. With the tunnel's dark history of decapitations and other unpleasant deaths what do you expect?

When the interior is foggy, sometimes you can see what looks like human figures standing on the old railroad bed up ahead, but when you get close there's nothing there. There have been sightings of Confederate and Union soldiers. In the evening, phantom campfires begin to appear on the hillside. The fires will disappear if someone moves in too close. People have reported seeing the legs of soldiers moving around the edge of the campfires.

People have reported seeing lights like that of lantern lights along with hearing ghostly screams. Headless ghosts have been seen lurking around the tunnel. The ghosts of marching Confederate soldiers are occasionally seen on the battlefield. Some of the bloodiest battles in American history were fought there.

A shape began to take form in the entrance of the tunnel, and as a group of people got closer to it, it just vanished. The smell of rotting human flesh can sometimes be smelled. Some people in the area can smell it while others don't. The scent has come to be known as the death smell. One person witnessed a Confederate soldier walking along a picket fence. Footsteps are often heard when no one is there.

On one occasion, a group of reenactors saw a soldier's ghost walk around their camp when a circular fog surrounded the camp. One night, a Confederate soldier walked out of a fog toward a reenactor. The reenactor thought it was one of his buddies until it disappeared before reaching him.

On one occasion, a group saw a Union soldier lying beside the road at the campsite. He had his head lying on his pack. He had apparently fallen asleep. They carefully passed by him, trying not to wake him. When they looked back, he had vanished. People have reported seeing flickering lights around the tunnel.

CURSED PILLAR

The cursed pillar was a landmark standing near the remains of the Old Farmers Market in Augusta, Georgia. It stood from 1830 until the market was destroyed by a freak winter tornado on February 7, 1878. The following year, the pillar was moved to the opposite corner of Fifth Street. It was used to display advertisements by Theodore Eye's Broad Street Grocery.

According to the legend and local folklore, a traveling preacher wanted to preach next to the pillar, but the locals didn't want him to so they talked to the authorities about it. The local authorities forbid him that right. The preacher declared that the market would be destroyed by a great wind and whoever tried to move the pillar would be struck dead. A freak winter tornado set down in the middle of the market on February 7, 1878, destroying the market. The only thing left standing was the pillar.

In 1930 the City of Augusta hired a press agency, the New York–based firm of Aulockhart International, to create and publish an advertising campaign aimed at attracting tourists. They published a ghost story about the pillar in newspapers across the United States. The story referred to the pillar as the haunted pillar.

In 1931, Augusta mayor Will Jennings hired a press agent to spread the word of the curse. There are accounts up until the late 1950s telling of the unfortunate highway workers that were struck by lightning bolts out of a clear blue sky and those crushed by their machinery when they attempted to

move the pillar. Local folklore says that if anyone touches the pillar they will perish shortly after or be doomed forever.

A man said he would knock it down. He got a sledgehammer and started whacking away at the pillar. The police were called, and the man was arrested.

On December 17, 2016, the pillar was destroyed in a car collision. The driver was never caught. On May 8, 2017, the pillar was still gone, replaced by an orange construction barrel.

The Augusta Convention and Visitors Bureau started taking up funds to help with the restoration. At the time of this writing, it has not yet been restored. The pillar sat on the sidewalk where Broad Street and Fifth Street meet.

NUCLEAR AIRCRAFT LABORATORY

The remains of one of America's first radiation testing grounds rest silent in a Georgia forest. Deep in the woods of Georgia's Dawson Forest lay the remains of what was once a nuclear testing facility from the early 1950s, code name Air Force Plant No. 67. This plant was a joint effort between the U.S. Air Force and Lockheed Martin's Weapons manufacturing.

During its active years, the plant would fire up a small nuclear reactor and irradiate various pieces of military equipment and the surrounding forest to observe the effects it had on the equipment and the surrounding forest. The test was to see if a nuclear-powered airplane was feasible. Reports say the reactor was unshielded. The personnel would have to go into underground bunkers or tunnels when the nuclear reactor was turned on. The radiation caused severe damage to the surrounding forest.

The exact nature of what was going on at the top-secret facility is still top secret. The plant was closed and much of it dismantled in 1971. The only thing left behind is concrete pilings, husks and the flat foundations of the buildings. In its working days, the plant was spread over thousands of acres and went five stories underground. Some of the walls were five-foot-thick concrete. There is one building left from the plant. The hot cell building still remains intact. The doors, windows and any other access points are sealed up. Because of contamination concerns, the hot cell building is surrounded by two fences. The entrances to the underground tunnels were destroyed to keep people out. No radiation is found around the old, abandoned plant or in the nearby forest.

One source says that live animals and two humans were deliberately exposed to different kinds of radiation for prolonged periods of time. The two humans were known as SX66 and SX67. SX66 died after a few weeks. SX67 experienced different effects. The cells began to grow rapidly. SX67's eyes began to grow, and the pupils were disproportionate to normal eyes. The white part of the eyes seemed to almost glow green in the dark. The bones were extremely dense. SX67 couldn't swim because of the weight of its body. It had thick, gray, rubbery skin. SX67 was sealed in a large containment building, and it was assumed that SX67 died.

One report states that a man was murdered in the forest in the mid-1990s, and the crime is still unsolved. In 2005, a woman's head was found hanging from a tree. People have ventured into the forest never to be heard from again. None of these incidents could be confirmed.

Do not trespass, it is still restricted property.

TYBEE ISLAND NUCLEAR BOMB

On February 5, 1958, Tybee Island narrowly escaped being completely destroyed by a nuclear bomb. A B-47 Air Force bomber piloted by Colonel Howard Richardson dropped a nuclear bomb into the water off the coast of Tybee Island after colliding with an F-18 fighter jet during a training mission. Richardson was afraid the bomb would break loose from his plane when he landed. Richardson dropped the bomb in the water before he made an emergency landing at Hunter Air Force base outside Savannah, Georgia. The 7,100-pound bomb lies somewhere on the bottom of Wassaw Sound. The nuclear bomb has an explosive power one hundred times greater than the bomb dropped on Hiroshima, Japan, in World War II. The U.S. Air Force said the device lacked a plutonium trigger, rendering it incapable of exploding.

The fighter jet's pilot, Lieutenant Clarence Stewart out of Charleston, South Carolina, didn't see the B-47 bomber on his radar. Lieutenant Stewart descended directly onto Richardson's B-47 bomber. The midair collision ripped the left wing off the F-18 fighter jet and damaged the fuel tanks on the B-47. Stewart was in serious trouble. With no other choice, Lieutenant Stewart ejected at thirty-five thousand feet into an outside temperature of fifty degrees below zero and landed safely in the Savannah River swamp on the South Carolina side. Eventually, Stewart heard an approaching airplane. Stewart's frostbitten fingers due to the high-altitude cold weren't working very well. When he tried to fire his flare gun, he almost shot his toes off. The exploding flare signaled a ranger, who thought

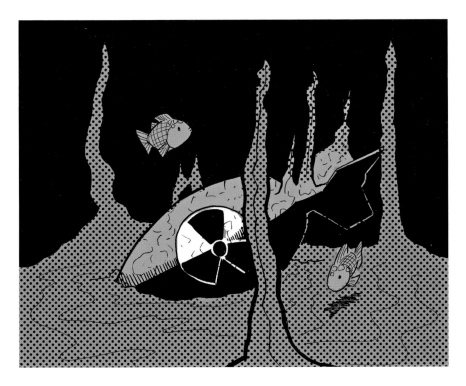

Stewart was a poacher. When the ranger found Stewart and found that he was an Air Force pilot, he drove Stewart to a nearby hospital, where he was given medical attention. He was then picked up by a helicopter and returned to Charleston Air Force Base.

The U.S. Navy searched for the bomb for more than two months before calling off the search. The bomb has never been found. If left undisturbed, it poses no threat. The question should be what happens if the bomb is disturbed by something other than a recovery attempt?

Air Force records indicate the Mark 15 bomb bore the serial number 47782 on it. The bomb contained four hundred pounds of high explosives and an undisclosed amount of enriched uranium, another nuclear material. The Mark 15 bomb is capable of incinerating everything within a 5-mile radius and would create a 160-mil- high plume of radioactive fallout.

In June 2005, after another extensive search, the federal government said again the bomb is irretrievably lost. The case of the lost nuclear bomb is officially closed. Tybee Island residents haven't forgotten about the deadly bomb lying quietly of the coast.

Sometime around 1960, Bubba Smith was fishing in front of Tybee's public fishing pier when he snagged something in his fishing net that was so heavy he couldn't raise it. Bubba tried to save his net by hiring a local diver to dive down and see what was caught in his net. The diver surfaced and told Bubba that he had caught a bomb. Bubba cut his net loose and left it right there. He shared his story with a few close friends before he went to his reward in 2006.

GLOW WORMS

Hawkinsville is a small town in Pulaski County with a population of fewer than ten thousand residents. It is famous for harness horses, large freight animals. Underground lives a mysterious kind of earthworm. This earthworm grows up to two feet long and secretes a sticky slime that glows blue in the dark.

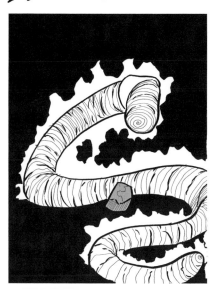

This makes these slithering little creatures different from the rest of the earthworms. This slime is made up of the same chemical that lights up lightning bugs. Scientists have named it *Diplocardia longa*.

Locals say you can hammer a stake into the ground, causing vibrations that attract the worms. The worms will come to the surface. This process is called grunting. Glow worms are also found in New Zealand and Australia.

CHRIST CHURCH CEMETERY LIGHT

A 275-year-old Episcopal church on St. Simons Island is one of America's oldest churches. It is a historic landmark dating back to the 1730s, when James Oglethorpe and the first English settlers arrived on what is now St. Simons Island, Georgia.

The cemetery predates the church by about five years. There's a ghostly legend that goes with the burying ground. At some point during the antebellum years, a young woman with a fear of the dark died and was buried in the Christ Church Cemetery. Her husband began bringing a candle to her grave as darkness neared. He would bring the candle every day until his death.

For years, people who visited the graveyard at night would see a flickering light inside the graveyard. Is her husband still bringing a candle to his wife's grave even after his own death?

Today, progress has obliterated the view of the light. A brick wall was built along Frederica Road, and at night spotlights shine on the church. Some say that even today the light can sometimes be seen outside the wall.

OLD CANDLER HOSPITAL

The Old Candler Hospital was Georgia's first hospital. It is located in Savannah and was chartered in 1804. It is recognized as the second oldest continuously operating hospital in the United States. The Old Candler Hospital was known for its outstanding patient care. In 1980, the Candler Hospital moved to its current location on Reynolds Street. In 1997, Candler Hospital entered into a joint operating agreement with St. Joseph's Hospital and together formed St. Joseph's/Candler, the region's largest and most experienced healthcare provider. The hospital was one of a kind in its day. Sadly, the Old Candler Hospital now lies in ruins. Nature is reclaiming it. One source says what is left of the Old Candler Hospital has been remodeled and is presently being used as a law school.

In 1876, one of the largest yellow fever epidemics hit the city of Savannah. During this outbreak, there were thousands of people that fell victim to the yellow fever and died in the Candler Hospital. Tunnels were dug under the hospital, and secret burials were made throughout the tunnel. It is said that the tunnel was a place to put the victims of yellow fever to keep from bringing them out in the public. There were no exits to the tunnels. The story goes that the tunnels ran from the hospital out under Forsyth Park.

An article in the *Savannah Morning News* dated 1884 discusses how there was going to be an underground tunnel to replace the above ground morgue. Another story about the tunnel goes like this: when the tunnel was filled with dead bodies, in the dark of night horse-drawn wagons

would secretly carry off the bodies to be buried elsewhere. Other rumors surrounding the Old Candler Hospital involved shock treatment used in the psychiatric ward and other horrifying procedures that were dubbed as treatments.

The tunnel is reported to be a hotbed of strange happenings, including people seeing orbs, apparitions and unexplained noises. The Candler Hospital also served as a prisoner-of-war camp for Union soldiers. Images of ghost soldiers have been seen in and around the Old Candler Hospital. When people are investigating the tunnel, light sources shut off for no reason.

The Old Candler Hospital is home to the nearly three-hundred-year-old Candler Oak Tree, better known as the hanging tree. Sometimes at night you can get a glimpse of the apparition of a person hanging from the branches of the old oak tree. The tree is sixteen feet in circumference on the ground.

CANDLER HISTORICAL MARKER INSCRIPTION

Georgia's first hospital, Candler is the second-oldest continuously operating hospital in the United States. Its history began in the 1730s when Methodist missionary George Whitfield brought medicines to treat sick seamen and the poor. Chartered in 1804 as a seaman's hospital and poor house, it was later incorporated in 1808 under the name Savannah Poor House and Hospital Society. In 1819, the hospital moved to Gaston Street, where it remained for 160 years. After Union forces occupied Savannah, the building served as a Union Hospital until 1866. Renamed the Savannah Hospital in 1872, it later housed the city's first nursing school, which opened in 1902. The Methodist Church purchased the hospital in 1930, renaming it for Bishop Warren A. Candler. In 1960, the hospital joined forces with the country's oldest women's hospital, Mary Telfair. In 1978, groundbreaking ceremonies were held on this site and the facility was completed in October 1980. In 1992, it was renamed Candler Hospital and in 1997, the hospital entered a joint operating agreement with St. Joseph's Hospital, forming St. Joseph's Candler Health System.

JEKYLL ISLAND CLUB HOTEL

Jekyll Island is a place where time just seems to stand still. Jekyll Island is home to a haunted hotel, the Jekyll Island Club Hotel. The exclusive Jekyll Island Club opened in 1888 and had only one hundred members, made up of America's rich and famous, such as Joseph Pulitzer, J.P. Morgan, William Rockefeller and William K. Vanderbilt, just to name a few. Lloyd Aspinwell was elected president of the club and eagerly awaited its grand opening. Aspinwell suddenly died without seeing the grand opening.

Several historic events took place at the Jekyll Island Club. Legislation that outlined the formation of the Federal Reserve was drafted here in 1910. The first transcontinental phone call from the president of American Telephone and Telegraph (A&T), Theodore Vail, to Woodrow Wilson, Alexander Graham Bell and Thomas A. Watson was made in 1915. When the members of the club weren't busy, they were hunting or playing golf.

Once the great Depression started, the Jekyll Island Club fell on hard times. World War II didn't help the club any. The Jekyll Island Club couldn't survive and had to close its doors in 1942.

The State of Georgia bought Jekyll Island Club in 1947 and started operating it as a private hotel in the 1980s. It is still run as a hotel today. It is part of the Jekyll Island National Landmark Historic District.

The Jekyll Island Club Hotel, like many other old places, occasionally has a visitor from the past. One such visitor is Samuel Spencer. Spencer, a

railroad magnate with the Southern Railroad, had a second-floor apartment in the annex building. He was accidently struck and killed by one of his own trains in 1906. From time to time, Spencer visits apartment 8 in the annex to enjoy a cup of coffee and catch up on the news in the *Wall Street Journal*. Guests in apartment 8 keep reporting that their coffee cups and newspapers were rearranged.

Another of their unearthly visitors is Lloyd Aspinwall, whose ghost has been seen walking along the riverfront veranda with his hands clasped behind his back. In 1985, when the hotel was renovated, the veranda was glassed in and renamed the Aspinwall Room.

A bellhop from the 1920s keeps returning. Employees claim there have been times when they returned dry cleaning to a wedding party guest and knocked on the door, but nobody answered. They leave the clothes on the outside and go down the hall only to find the clothes missing when they return to the room. The guests relate that a bellhop in an old-fashioned uniform knocked on the door, and when they answered it, the bellhop handed them the clothes before vanishing. Other guests have seen him walking the halls with his pillbox hat and striped pants.

GEORGIA WEREWOLF GIRL

Emily Isabella Burt, the Georgia Werewolf Girl, was a resident of Talbot County, a rural county in southwest Georgia. Emily Isabella was born on July 29, 1841, to Mildred Owen Burt in an area known as Pleasant Hill. Her family was wealthy, and they were prominent members of the town of Woodland. There were four children: Sarah, Mildred, Emily Isabella and Joel.

The untimely death of her husband left thirty-seven-year-old Mildred Own Burt to care for the children alone, but she did inherit a nice estate. Instead of worrying over the children she sent them to Europe so they could get a good education.

When Emily Isabella returned home from abroad she began complaining of insomnia. She would slip out in the middle of the night without telling anyone. Her mother couldn't shake the feeling that something was wrong with Isabella.

The legend says that the beau of one of Isabella's sisters told the Burts that something was killing the rancher's sheep. A man named Gorman shared stories of the sheep killings and relayed that some of his cattle had also been killed in the same way. Gorman reported to the Burt family that he was putting together a posse and they were going to hunt down and kill the animal that was responsible for the deaths of their livestock. The men's first thought was it was a gray wolf, but the animal tracks were unknown to them. They also posted armed men around their livestock. The animals were never eaten, just killed.

Professional hunters were brought in. Several people shot at the animal from a distance but were never able to kill it. One farmer that had lost a lot of his livestock offered a $200 reward to anyone who killed the animal.

Another farmer met a new settler in the area. They were discussing the problem that the farmers were facing, and the newcomer said that back in Bohemia they had the same problem. The new settler told the farmer the story of the werewolf. He gave the farmer his silver cross and told him to melt it down and make bullets out of it. That's the only way you can kill a werewolf. The farmers melted it down and made bullets for their rifles.

One night, a farmer shot an animal with one of his silver bullets. The animal let out a piercing scream that sounded more like a woman than an animal. The men who were posted ran to see if the animal had been killed. They found the left front paw of the beast, which had been shot off. The animal killings stopped.

Years later, the town doctor revealed that on the night of the shooting he had bandaged a young woman's arm from a wound that looked like her hand had been shot off.

After Isabella was patched up, Mildred Burt sent her to Paris, where she visited a doctor that specialized in lycanthropy. Isabella returned to her home several years later and lived out the rest of her life in peace.

At the time of Emily Isabella's death, she was living with her sister in Marietta, Georgia. She was loved and well respected in Talbot and Cobb Counties. In 1911, Isabella Burt died at the age of seventy. She was laid to rest in holy ground in the Owen and Holmes Cemetery in Talbot County, Georgia.

Her obituary reads "Miss Emily Burt of Midland Georgia died at the home of Mrs. Benson in Marietta Georgia Sunday June 18, 1911. Her remains were brought to Woodland for burial on Tuesday June 20, 1911."

While researching this story, I was not able to find any documentation substantiating this tale. The graveyard is on private property. Do not trespass. Get permission before you go.

MYSTERIOUS LAKE LANIER

T he birth of Lake Sidney Lanier, referred to simply as Lake Lanier, actually began with the purchase of a one-hundred-acre farm from river ferry operator Henry Shadburn in 1948. The land purchase was the beginning of the start of a dam project on the Chattahoochee River to provide the city of Atlanta with hydroelectricity. The Buford Dam on the Chattahoochee River was completed in 1956. It took five years for the lake to reach its full pool depth of 1,072 feet above sea level. It was completed at a cost of $45 million. Today, its economic impact exceeds $5 billion annually, based on a study in 2000 by the Marine Trade Association of Metropolitan Atlanta.

The U.S. Government ravenously purchased land from private companies, farmers and everyone else living in the area that would be under water. The government bought over 50,000 acres of farmland and wilderness, moved more than 250 families and 15 businesses and relocated 20 cemeteries—along with their corpses.

The spread of the water covered towns, houses, farmland, bridges, historical landmarks, roads, forests and other lakes. Lying in the northern part of Georgia, sprawled out among the foothills and the mountains was a 26-mile, 258-foot-deep lake at its deepest part, with an area of 59 square miles and 692 miles of shoreline. Lake Lanier is the largest lake in Georgia, and it even has a chain of islands that were large hills before the lake was made.

Lake Lanier is one of Georgia's top tourist attractions with more than eight million visitors a year. It has 68 parks and recreation areas, 12 campgrounds, more than 1,200 campsites and 10 full-service marinas with restaurants, gas and boat storage.

The eerie history of the underwater ghost towns, ghost ships and desecrated cemeteries are not the only strange things about Lake Lanier. Lake Lanier has accumulated a rather sinister reputation for drowning deaths. There have been a large number of deaths from boating accidents; drivers lose control of their vehicles and run off the road and into the lake. It was estimated that 675 people died lake-related deaths in 2017.

There are a number of ghost stories about Lake Lanier. One story is about the Lady of the Lake. The Lady of the Lake is said to walk along the Dawsonville Highway Bridge, or the Lanier Bridge. She is seen wearing a blue dress and missing both hands. Could this be the ghost of Delia Parker Young, who went missing after she and her friend Susie Roberts left a gas station without paying for their gas? Could she be looking for her hands? Her body was found by a fisherman when it floated to the surface. It was in November 1990, when construction on the new Lanier Bridge expansion was underway, that crews found Roberts's car. Roberts was identified by her belongings. The two girls were buried side by side.

Another ghost is named Agnes. There are contradictory stories about her. One says she hanged herself at the university. Another says she drowned. There is not much on Agnes. Another story is that in 1903 there was an accident in that area in which eighty-eight people died. Could they be haunting the lake?

Boats have been reported hitting things in the water when there's nothing there. Boats have capsized for no apparent reason. Some swimmers reported being pulled under the water or just being held there without any control. There have been reports of a ghostly raft appearing and disappearing at night. For decades, the raft with its ghostly person on board guiding the raft with a pole has been seen. There is a light that looks like a lantern hanging from a pole on the raft.

There have been reports of rogue waves coming out of nowhere without warning and moving across the surface of the lake. Local fisherman and divers have reported giant catfish five to seven feet long. There have been reports of then attacking swimmers and divers. The giant catfish are attracted to the deep water near the dam.

OKEFENOKEE SWAMP

The Okefenokee Swamp, which straddles Georgia and Florida, is one of the largest in the world. It is home to deadly quicksand, venomous snakes, alligators and many strange things. The Okefenokee Swamp covers roughly 700 square miles. It is a 38-by-25-mile area and 438,000 thousand acres of freshwater swamp. The majority of the Okefenokee Swamp is protected by the Okefenokee National Refuge and the Okefenokee Wilderness. The swamp was once part of the ocean floor. The ocean waters emptied into the Gulf of Mexico and the Atlantic Ocean, leaving the Okefenokee Swamp.

In 1829, a group of men had a fatal encounter with what can only be described as a big, hairy creature. Two men who dared to explore deep into the swamp found footprints eighteen inches long and nine inches wide. After telling others about the footprints, a group of seven men decided to go hunt down and kill the creature that made the tracks. After a couple of weeks, the group found the creature's tracks. Only seconds after the men started to make camp, the creature attacked the men. The creature stood an estimated thirteen feet tall and was covered with hair. The hunters started shooting at the creature. Badly wounded, the creature still continued the attack on the men, killing five of the seven hunters. After it was all over, the creature, mortally wounded, let out a scream that scared the two men. Fearing the scream would call more creatures, the two surviving men left their five dead friends behind and made a hasty retreat. This story cannot be verified. The story supposedly appeared in the *Milledgeville Georgia Statesman* newspaper in either January or February 1829. There have been many sightings of Bigfoot in the Okefenokee Swamp.

There have been numerous UFO sightings and mysterious lights in the swamp over the years. In May 1998, a UFO was spotted on the east side of the swamp. It was described as a large, shiny black object that hovered for a few minutes before breaking into smaller objects that flew in many different directions.

The local legend around the Okefenokee Swamp says that Spanish explorers who went into the swamp swore that the forest turned into giant warriors and shot arrows at them. On stormy nights, ghost ships slip up the St. Marys River. Skeleton crews sail the boats up this waterway to unload their forbidden cargo of slaves on the sandbars.

In 1920, a railroad was built to move lumber out of the swamp. The railroad construction workers found it necessary to cut through a half moon–shaped Indian mound on Floyds Island. The workers unearthed several skeletons of giant men.

In the 1930s, a fisherman fishing near the railroad tracks at Henson Creek fell asleep one night using the rails as a pillow. A train appeared. The train sounded its whistle, but the fisherman didn't move. The story goes that a ghostly body can be seen walking along the tracks and swinging a lantern. Is this the ghost of the headless man looking for his head?

In January 1998, on Trail Ridge a person vacationing and taking a hike near the boardwalk heard the sounds of Indian drums in the piney woods. The vacationer, looking around, saw the ghosts of Indians carrying objects and walking in a single-file line heading south on the ridge. People marvel at how the ground and trees shake and tremble when you stomp on the ground around them.

JIMMY CARTER'S UFO SIGHTING

James Earl "Jimmy" Carter Jr. was born on October 1, 1924, in Plains, Georgia. Carter grew up in the nearby community of Archery, Georgia, but attended school in Plains, where he graduated. He then attended Georgia Southwestern College and the Georgia Institute of Technology. He joined the navy, where he received a bachelor's degree from the U.S. Naval Academy.

During his career in the U.S. Navy, Carter went on to become a submariner. He served in this capacity in the Atlantic and the Pacific fleets and rose to the rank of lieutenant. Carter was chosen for the nuclear submarine program and assigned to Schenectady, New York. He took graduated studies at the Union College in reactor technology and nuclear physics. He served on the second nuclear submarine, the *Seawolf.*

On July 7, 1946, he married Rosalynn Smith of Plains, Georgia. In 1962, he won election to the Georgia Senate. On January 12, 1971, Carter became Georgia's seventy-sixth governor.

UFO sightings are one of those polarizing things people have different opinions of. There are those who are firm believers and nothing said can change their minds. There are those who think, *well maybe something does exist.* There are those who think the idea of UFOs is ridiculous. Many think that the people who believe in UFOs are some kind of nuts.

Some reports of sightings have come from less-than-credible sources. But then there are many sightings that come from credible sources, like Jimmy Carter.

Carter's sighting occurred in 1969, when he was on his way to give a speech at the local Lion's Club in the town of Leary, Georgia. Carter didn't report the UFO sighting at that time. In 1973, while governor, he was asked by the International UFO Bureau in Oklahoma City, Oklahoma, if he would give a statement about UFOs. He filed a report about his UFO experience with the International UFO Bureau in Oklahoma City.

Carter was standing outside the Lion's Club at about 7:30 p.m. with about ten to twenty people when he became aware of a strange object in the sky moving toward them from the west. It stopped and hovered over a stand of pine trees. The object hovered about thirty degrees above the horizon and then moved off into the distance and disappeared. Carter described the object as bright, about the size of the moon and changing colors from blue to red and then back to white. It was in view for about ten minutes.

This report triggered an investigation. Those working on the project could not get to the bottom of what Carter had seen. The final report was that the investigation was inconclusive. Some believe it was the planet Venus or a weather balloon.

On December 12, 1974, Carter announced he was running for president of the United States of America. He was elected on November 2, 1976, and served as president from January 20, 1977, to January 20, 1981.

When he became president-elect, he approached the director of the CIA, George H.W. Bush, to inquire if the CIA knew anything about extraterrestrials and UFOs. Director Bush refused to answer Carter's questions. Carter reportedly said, "If I become president, I'll make every piece of information this country has about UFO sightings available to the public and scientists." After assuming office, Carter said that publishing documents of that sort could have an effect on issues of national security.

On December 10, 2002, the Norwegian Nobel Committee awarded Carter the Nobel Peace Prize.

WARNER ROBINS UFOs

October 17, 1973, is a day that the citizens of Georgia will never forget. It was around 9:00 p.m. when hundreds of Georgia residents, many of whom were law enforcement, witnessed strange lights that maneuvered across the sky. Shortly after the sky show, two unidentified objects made a spectacular impact with the ground.

In another incident, a diving UFO ran two military policemen off the road. Reports of alien spacecrafts from across the state were filed with local and state authorities. The most intense wave of UFO sightings in American history had begun in Georgia. On the night of October 17, the UFOs reached Warner Robins, and two UFO reports were received by the local and county authorities. There were two separate incidents.

At 9:00 p.m., Lawrence Smith, Peggy Stepp and Stepp's daughter Kathy Stepp spotted a large, cigar-shaped UFO about one hundred feet above the ground. The trio followed the UFO down Dunbar and Bateman Roads. Suddenly, there were two UFOs, and they were getting close. The UFOs were emitting a humming sound. The crafts were about the size of a house. The UFOs had red, green and blue lights. Smith was trying to get to a more populated area. Kathy screamed, "There's one behind us." The UFO got above the car and shone a bright light on them. Then it was gone in a flash. Smith called the Houston County Sheriff's Department at 9:30 p.m. and reported the UFO incidents.

Corporal Bobby Fisher was dispatched to investigate a UFO sighting near Elberta and Dunbar Roads. As Fisher reached the old Houston

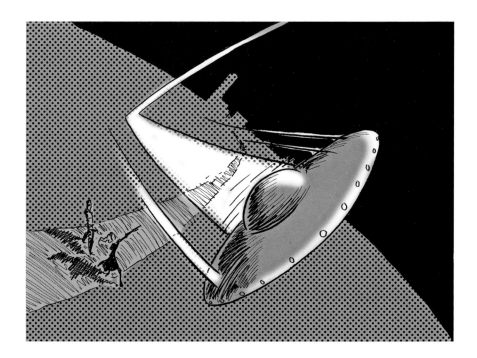

County fairgrounds at 9:57 p.m., he saw the same object reported by Smith hovering above the trees. It flew off in a westerly direction. Fisher immediately began a pursuit of the UFO and overtook it at Dunbar Road. The UFO stopped above Fisher's car. Fisher got out of the car and looked up at the UFO. The UFO was about one hundred feet above Fisher. While Fisher was on the radio trying to get some backup, the UFO flew off at an extremely high rate of speed.

Around this time, thousands of Central Georgia residents reported seeing the UFOs. Some of those were easily explained; two weather balloons were launched by the National Weather Service from Texas and Alabama. The balloons measured 150 feet in diameter. The weather balloons drifted over Georgia at 55,000 feet. They were high enough to reflect sunlight after the sun had set. Two rockets were launched from Eglin Air Force Base in Florida, which released clouds of glowing red, green and yellow gasses at an altitude of six miles. (Why were these rockets releasing clouds of glowing red, green and yellow gasses?)

These two incidents could not explain the sightings by Smith, Stepp and Corporal Fisher. Warner Robins Police Department logged over four hundred calls reporting UFOs.

PATHWAY TO HEAVEN

On April 25, 2017, a tragic two-vehicle accident took the lives of three young girls from Gainesville, Georgia. Hannah Simmons, twenty-three, was taking her nine-month-old daughter, A'lannah, to the doctor for a routine checkup. Her friend Lauren Buteau, twenty-eight, was riding with them. Hannah Simmons lost control off the car and ran head on into a truck. Hannah Simmons, A'lannah and Lauren Buteau lost their lives in the tragic accident that day. The accident occurred on Georgia Route 347 near Gainesville, Georgia.

Anisa Gannon, nineteen, was on her way to work when she had to stop due to traffic backup. She snapped a picture of the accident scene to show her boss in case she was late. It wasn't until later when she showed the picture to her aunt Tara Noble that they discovered this picture wasn't an ordinary picture of two wrecked vehicles, fire trucks and emergency workers. There was something more in this photo. There was a beam of light shining from the wreckage up into the sky. Aunt Tara spotted the light and immediately thought it was a pathway to heaven. The beam of light appeared to contain two small orbs.

Following the tragedy, Gannon located and met with the two mothers of the victims involved in the wreck to show them the picture. Jodi Simmons, mother of Hannah and the baby girl's grandmother, told *Inside Edition* that she believed the picture shows a pathway to Heaven. When Dana Buteau, Lauren's mother, saw the picture, she believed all the girls went straight to Heaven. Both mothers said that the picture brought them a lot of peace. Jodi Simmons keeps a copy of the picture on top of her television so it's always in view.

A reporter with the local media got a hold of the picture and posted it in his station's Twitter feed, where it was picked up by *People* magazine.

The long beam of light that reaches down from the top of the picture to the wreck site looks similar to a crepuscular ray, which sometimes happen as beams of light shine through holes in a cloud cover. Meteorologist Christopher Dolce with weather.com said it doesn't appear to be one since the sky in the photo shows mostly clear conditions and it wouldn't be that vivid up close.

GEORGIA LIGHTNING BUGS

As young'uns growing up in South Carolina, we called them lightning bugs, but some people refer to them as fireflies. We'd chase them, and when we caught one, it would go into a mason jar with a lid on it that had holes poked in it with a nail. We always let them go before we went in for the night. I grew up just outside of Hemingway, where lightning bugs were an every-summer-night thing. They fly slow and are easy to catch.

Fireflies or lightning bugs, whichever you prefer, spend their first year as larvae buried under leaves on the ground. The larvae will eat grubs, worms, snails and many insects. The adult lightning bug will come out in the spring and live long enough to mate and lay eggs. Lightning bugs attract each other with their periodic signals. The lightning bugs make their light from a combination of three substances: luciferin, (named for the fallen angel Lucifer) that is the yellow pigment that glows; luciferase, an enzymatic catalyst; and ATP, a nucleotide that gives the energy to cut on the cells that emit the light. Lightning bugs have organs in the rear of their bodies that produce light. Lightning bugs are not bugs at all—they are, in reality, small beetles.

The males fly around and light up looking for a female. The females do not fly; they wait on the vegetation until a male of the same species comes along, and then she will signal him with her flash. The male lightning bug is sometimes the victim of a deadly hoax. Some species of predatory lightning bugs imitate flashes of another species. When the unsuspecting lightning bug flies to the perpetrator, it is eaten.

There are 170 species of lightning bugs in North America, and 56 of those are found in Georgia. Georgia has the most species of lightning bugs in the country. Just sit on your porch and watch the lightning bugs light up the world around you.

If you live in the country, you can expect to see an abundance of lightning bugs. On a warm summer day, you should be able to see these sparkly little critters. If you live in a light-polluted area, you may not have the pleasure of seeing any lightning bugs. You may have to go find a dark area in the country to see them. If you live in the country, just keep your eyes peeled for these wonders of nature.

Lightning bugs have many different names around the globe, such as glow flies, golden sparklers, moon bugs, blinkies and fire devils. There are several legends that swirl around these little wonders of nature. The Chinese once harbored the belief that these glowing bugs were created when they burned grass. The Japanese thought that the insects were ghosts of valiant warriors killed in defense of their homeland.

Beauty can be found in the tiniest of things. Be enchanted by the beauty of their flickering light, but remember, don't hurt them.

MYSTERIOUS CREATURE WASHES ASHORE

A mysterious sea creature that washed ashore in southeastern Georgia has puzzled marine biologists. Experts are divided on whether the creature is a hoax, a decaying animal or some undiscovered sea life.

Jeff Warren found the carcass washed up on the shore of Georgia's Wolf Island National Wildlife Refuge near Darien on Friday, March 16, 2018. Warren sent photos to several media outlets in Georgia.

National Geographic said it's not clear what the mysterious creature is or, for that matter, if we'll ever get a clear answer. At first, Warren thought it was a dead seal, but when he took a closer look, it appeared to be a Loch Ness–type monster. The body's long neck and small head reminded locals of the Altamaha-ha, Georgia's version of Scotland's Nessie.

Chantel Audran of Tybee Island Marine Science Center said it looks like a frilled shark. Tara Cox, associate professor of marine science at Savannah State University, said it may be a decomposing basking shark. Mark Dodd of the Georgia Department of Natural Resources seconded Audran's guess. Dwight Gale and George Gale, two shrimp boat captains, thought it could be a sturgeon shark. Local marine scientists say it's some type of shark. Other marine scientists also considered it a decaying whale or an oarfish. The body of the sea monster was not recovered, nor were samples taken from it.

At Skippers Fish Camp in Darien, Georgia, they call it Ally, a reference to Altamaha-ha, the Georgia coast's version of Scotland's Loch Ness Monster. Live Science said it was possible, but unlikely, that the odd beast is a previously unknown deep-sea animal.

Not everyone ruled out a hoax, but if it was a hoax, whoever did it did a good job. Marine experts don't know what to make of the photos and video taken by Warren—some expressed skepticism alongside of awe.

Uno Garter, a scientific illustrator and president of the American Cetacean Society, said it's not a cetacean (a group that includes whales, dolphins and porpoises). Garter said it did not look like any kind of marine mammal, oarfish or type of eel.

John "Crawfish" Crawford, a naturalist at the University of Georgia Marine Extension and Georgia Sea Grant, believed the sea creature was a constructed model of a baby Altamaha-ha. Without an examination of the actual carcass, the jury is still out on the sea monster.

THE MYSTERY OF ALTAMAHA-HA

Since the mid-1500s, there have been rumors of something haunting the waters of Georgia's Altamaha River. Near the mouth of the Altamaha River in southeastern Georgia is believed to be a hissing sea or river monster called Altamaha-ha, or Altie for short. Local legend says that a twenty-plus-foot-long water serpent lives in one of the largest rivers in Georgia. The river empties into the Atlantic Ocean and has one of the largest river basins in the country. The Altamaha River runs 137 miles, joining up with three tributaries: the Ocmulgee, the Oconee and the Ohoopee Rivers.

The strange creature is described as having a sturgeon-like body, including a bony ridge on top. It has front flappers, swims like a dolphin and has the snout of a crocodile with big protruding eyes and large, sharp teeth. It is a gray or green color with a whitish yellow underbelly.

Tales of the creature go back to the mid-1500s. Jacques Le Moyne, the first European artist in America, was illustrating the new world of the coast of Georgia. Le Moyne's renderings may well be the first documentation of the legendary creature that has continued to be seen in the Altamaha River.

The Muscogee tribe recorded sighting of a river creature. The Tama Indians told stories of a huge water serpent that hissed. Captain Delano and five others aboard the schooner *Eagle* reported seeing the creature off St. Simons Island just below the mouth of the Altamaha River where it empties into the Atlantic Ocean. The captain described it as being about seventy feet long and as big around as a barrel with the head of

an alligator. This was reported in the April 18, 1830 issue of the *Savannah Georgian* newspaper.

In the 1920s, settlers who rode the river reported sightings of a strange creature, as did a group of loggers. In the 1930s, a group of hunters reported seeing the creature. Other sightings included a Boy Scout troop in the 1940s. In the 1950s, two officials from the Reidsville State Prison reported a sighting. In the 1960s, 1970s and 1980, there were reports of fishermen and crabbers seeing the creature. In 1981, Altie gained national attention when a newspaper publisher saw it while fishing. A more recent sighting was from a man pulling a boat up the river near Brunswick in 2002. He reported seeing something over twenty feet long. The latest sighting was in March 2018.

Altie has been seen basking in the sun on the banks of the river, swimming casually and even reacting defensively when boaters got too close.

The legend is quite popular in McIntosh and Glynn Counties, which border the Altamaha River on the coast. With no evidence for scientists to study, the mystery of Altamaha-ha will continue to live on in Georgia.

OAKLAND CEMETERY

In the early days of Atlanta, city officials bought six acres of land in 1850 to be a public burial ground. It was originally called the Atlanta Graveyard or the City Burial Place. At that time, the city of Atlanta had a population of about 2,500 residents and was growing. It needed a graveyard to accommodate the burgeoning population. The graveyard was located southeast of the city. It was renamed in 1872 and was the beginning of what is known today as Oakland Cemetery. By 1872, the cemetery had expanded to forty-eight acres due to the casualties of the Civil War. The cemetery had to accommodate a large number of Civil War burials, both Confederate and Union. The oldest grave in Oakland Cemetery belongs to Agnes Wooding, who was buried there before the land was bought from her husband by the city of Atlanta. The first person buried in the cemetery after it was bought by the city of Atlanta was Dr. James Nissen, who passed away of an illness while visiting Atlanta.

Some Civil War battles were fought inside Oakland Cemetery. In the summer of 1864, the cemetery served as Confederate commander John B. Hood's headquarters. Oakland Cemetery became the final resting place for around seven thousand Confederate soldiers, with about three thousand of the soldiers unidentified. Union soldiers were also buried in the cemetery. There is a sixty-five-foot Confederate obelisk that was placed in the cemetery in 1870 honoring the Confederate soldiers that died in battle and were laid to rest there. There is another monument commemorating the unknown Confederate soldiers that died in the battle of Atlanta. Northeast of the obelisk is the Lion of Atlanta.

Oakland Cemetery is made up of several distinct areas. Jewish Flat and Jewish Hill are along the southern border. The land for Jewish Hill was acquired in 1878 and the Jewish Flat in 1892. This section has closely spaced markers. The Bell Tower Ridge, with its mausoleums and huge magnolias, along with the African American grounds' vernacular headstones lie on the northeastern eastern part of the property. Just beyond the African American grounds to the east is a sloping grassy hillside of about six acres known as the potter's field. Some graves are less than a foot apart and were marked with wooden headboards, which have succumbed to the elements over the years.

Many historic figures have been laid to rest in Oakland Cemetery. One of them is Maynard Jackson, the first African American mayor of Atlanta. Another mayor of Atlanta laid to rest there was Ivan Allen Jr. The grave of Margaret Mitchell, author of *Gone with the Wind*, is one of the cemetery's biggest tourism draws. James M. Calhoun is also interred there. He was an Atlanta mayor and is remembered for surrendering Atlanta to the Union army September 2, 1864.

In the late nineteenth century, families tended their loved ones' plots, creating an assortment of lovely gardens. Oakland Cemetery became a popular location for carriage rides. As the twentieth century arrived, residential and industrial development began surrounding Oakland Cemetery. As time passed, many graves lay unattended as descendants died or moved away and lost touch with their loved ones. Oakland began to deteriorate.

In 1976, Oakland Cemetery was listed in the National Register of Historic Places. This renewed the interest of the local people who would later become the Historic Oakland Foundation. This organization did fundraising and restoration projects and restored Oakland to a major tourist attraction. Oakland Cemetery has around fifty thousand visitors a year.

On March 14, 2008, a tornado passed through, waking Oakland Cemetery from its eternal sleep. The wind knocked down namesake oak trees, which fell on and broke fragile marble monuments. The angel Gabriel with his trumpet in hand waiting to summon the sleeping souls for judgment day was thrown to the ground by the strong winds. Hundreds of monuments and headstones were damaged by the tornado. Shortly after the tornado hit, the Historic Oakland Foundation went to work cleaning up and repairing the cemetery.

The Ghosts of Oakland

The most well-known ghostly occurrence is that of the roll call of the dead. People have reported hearing names being called out in a military-like roll call. They also heard responses to the names called out as if the soldiers were answering roll call. Some visitors have reported seeing a Union soldier hanging from a tree. Others have reported while visiting the cemetery in the middle of the night seeing Jasper Newton Smith rising out from his statue. People have also reported hearing a bugle call. People have heard an invisible sentry walking through the visitor's center at night. While there, visit the gift shop for an assortment of spooky books and gifts.

BONAVENTURE CEMETERY

Bonaventure Cemetery, located in Savannah, is one of the most visited cemeteries in the world. Bonaventure Cemetery is famous for its inhabitants both notable and unearthly. The cemetery is also famous for its beauty and its resting place beside the Wilmington River. The cemetery is a sculpture garden with towering obelisks, elaborate crypts, headstones carved with poetic epitaphs and realistic statues. These lie under huge old oak trees draped in Spanish moss and tree-lined roadways. Bonaventure Cemetery covers 160 acres.

Bonaventure Cemetery was developed on the historically significant site of Bonaventure Plantation. The site was bought for a private cemetery in 1846 and later became a public cemetery in 1907. Bonaventure was made famous for a picture of a statue on the cover of the bestselling book *Midnight in the Garden of Good and Evil* by John Berendt.

Many notable people are laid to rest in Bonaventure. These include Corinne Eliot (Eliott) Lawton, born on September 21, 1846. She was born into the wealthy family of Brigadier General Alexander Robert Lawton, Confederate States of America. On January 24, 1877, Corinne died in bed from an illness after five or six days surrounded by her family.

She was interred in Laurel Grove Cemetery first but was reinterred at Bonaventure Cemetery. Her epitaph reads "Allured to brighter worlds and led the way." The statue that was placed at her grave was created by Sicilian sculptor Benedetto Civiletti in his studio in Sicily in 1879. She is depicted as sitting below a cross and wearing a long gown with one shoulder bare. A garland of flowers has slipped from her hand, and she looks so sad. Her eyes don't have any pupils. The statue faces away from the family plot.

Corinne fell in love with a man her family thought was beneath her position in society. Her parents were dead set against her marrying a man who was less than acceptable for her. They made arrangements for her to marry a man of Savannah society. Corinne said she would never love him.

The legend goes that one day before the wedding, Corinne—heartbroken because she could not marry the man she loved—rode her father's best horse to the banks of the Savannah River. Heartbroken she leaped in the river and drowned.

Alexander R. Lawton's monument stands in the background overlooking the river. Lawton's monument is a life-size sculpture of Jesus Christ at Heaven's Gate. Lawton died in 1896.

Bonaventure is the final resting place of some well-known people, including singer–song writer Johnny Mercer, Georgia governor Edward Telfair, Jim Morrison, Oscar Wilde and novelist Conrad Aiken.

One of the more touching stories is the story of little Gracie Watson born in 1883, only six years old when she expired, who was laid to rest in 1889. She died just two days before Easter of pneumonia. A life-like sculpture of Gracie was commissioned by her father, and it sits on Gracie's grave.

Now here's one for you. There have been supposed sightings of the statue walking about the cemetery at night. People have reported seeing Gracie playing in Johnson Square. Some believe that if you place a quarter in the statue's hand and circle the statue three times, the coin will vanish, but with the statue's down-turned hands nothing can be placed inside. People who stood close to her grave have reported seeing the ghost of Gracie. The ghost has been seen sitting beside a tree, clutching a flower. The fence around Gracie's grave is always adorned with flowers, cards and toys.

Sounds of a baby crying can be heard near an infant's grave. Probably the most disturbing sound is the sound of a pack of dogs snarling and barking angrily. The dogs have never been seen.

MILLEDGEVILLE ORBS

Sometime in March 2019, something strange started happening at a residence in Milledgeville, Georgia. Orbs started appearing at the residence, and the security camera started recording them. The orbs appeared to be on a time schedule. They appeared about 8:30 p.m. about every forty-eight hours.

The orbs seemed to pause their movements when they came in contact with metal. A second orb was seen coming out of the carport area. It elevated a little, paused, and then went back into the carport.

When the third orb showed up, it came in fast, curling downward into a window. The fourth orb came in slowly, going into the carport and then back out and upward. The fifth was two orbs. The sixth orb seemed to be leaving. No details were given on additional orbs.

GRAVITY HILL

There are places that seem to defy the laws of physics. There is one such place in Bonaire, Georgia, called Gravity Hill. This mysterious place has drawn visitors and curiosity seekers to it for many years. The story is a bit of a legend in the Bonaire community.

The legendary Gravity Hill can easily be reached by following State Road 96 East across the Ocmulgee River to the intersection of US Route 129. Turn left and pass over the first hill. Continue on until you get to the bottom of the next hill, then stop. Put your car in neutral, and your vehicle will suddenly appear to defy gravity by rolling uphill. It will roll on its own to the top of the hill.

There is a legend that a witch is buried near the hill, about three hundred yards from Gravity Hill. There is evidence of a grave in the swamp marked with a pile of stones five feet high. That is believed to be the witch's grave. Since the witch couldn't be buried in holy ground in a church cemetery, the people took her body into the swamp and laid her to rest there.

The legend says that the witch extracted a toll from travelers on this road more than two hundred years ago. If she was paid, she would let them cross the hill. There's no record of what she did if they didn't pay. The locals left her alone to collect her toll. The locals asked her for help only once, and that was during a drought. The witch expired in 1850.

Is Gravity Hill an optical illusion? Check it out from the opposite side of the hill. You will see that the cars are actually rolling downhill. Regardless, try it.

THE WOG

The Wog is a mysterious creature that roamed the Nodoroc mud volcano site and surrounding areas near Winder, Georgia. The Wog is a black wolf-like creature with a long, forked tongue and huge red eyes. It's about the size of a small horse with a head resembling that of a bear. It has huge front legs and smaller back legs. It has a huge bushy black tail with white fur at the end and big white teeth. Its tail has been described as being in constant motion. The very existence of the Wog has been disputed.

The Wog was first seen around 1809 near what is now called Winder. It has been seen in Jackson and Barrow Counties. The Indians told the first white settlers that as long as you left the Wog alone it would not harm anyone. They said it was the devil. All farm animals were scared of the Wog and would make a hasty retreat when the Wog would come around. The legend says that the Wog will attack only when threatened. It roams the area looking for small animals to feed on.

The legend tells us that the Wog protects what was once or still is a mud volcano called the Nodoroc. The Nodoroc is an old boggy bubbling pond near the town of Winder, Georgia. Nodoroc is purportedly a Creek word meaning "gateway to hell." The area is several acres full of bubbling bluish mud-like sludge. The center has the appearance of boiling water. Trees or other vegetation don't grow very well in that area.

The Creek Indians of the 1800s built a stone altar at the mud volcano where they executed prisoners and tossed their bodies into the bog to suffer there for eternity. People were to be abandoned in the Nodoroc for the worst

crimes. The legend says that a woman murdered and ate her child and was thrown into the Nodoroc for her crime. Some people say that you can still hear her cries of terror and horrific pain in the Nodoroc area.

Some sources say that geologists have studied the watery bog since around 1800. The geological origin of the mud volcano is still a mystery. The first European explorers to visit the Nodoroc say that it burned and dissolved anything they threw into it. Others say that geologists have never studied the bog.

There are potentially huge numbers of Pleistocene fossils in the now dormant mud volcano dating back as far as thirty thousand years.

COLLEY CASTLE AKA BONNIE CASTLE

Originally, Grantville was known as Calico Corners. The history of Grantville is tied to the railroads and an Atlantan named Lemuel P Grant. Grant was the chief engineer of the Atlanta and West Point Railroad, which ran straight through town.

The first house built in Grantville was the J.R. Cotton house (1894). In 1896, J.W. Colley built the Colley House, which later became known as Bonnie Castle. Colley and his wife, affectionately known as Miss Love, designed the edifice. The Colley House was built with local bricks and granite from Stone Mountain, and the wood used was heart pine. The Colley house was a twenty-room mansion representing Victoriana at its finest.

Colley started textile mills and continued to buy up land. He was also a banker in the area. The Colleys were big in the social and political life in Coweta County in the early 1900s. The Colley house remained in the Colley family until 1881, when Patti and Darwin Palmer bought it and eventually named it Bonnie Castle.

The Palmers turned the Colley House into a bed-and-breakfast in 1993. This historic home has seen its share of important guests over the years, including Franklin Roosevelt, Madam Chiang Kai-Shek and Jimmy Carter, just to name a few.

The tower museum displays artifacts and memorabilia belonging to the original owners.

Bonnie Castle offers four bedrooms, two private baths, two guest rooms and a separate sitting area. The Prophet's room is the one-bed chamber

used to provide a place for traveling preachers. The Civil War suite, located in the turret, is a delightful suite for children. It includes two Civil War hospital beds.

Now a word about the ghosts of Bonnie Castle. The first ghost is called Mary. Mary hates electricity. Mary will randomly turn it on and off as she pleases. In other ghostly happenings, cameras will turn themselves on and off. The owners say it's just Mary. There is a ghost cat that has been seen on the grounds over the past few decades. There are reports of a man who continues to visit the property, claiming to be the original owner. Weird apparitions keep appearing in the windows, and doors are reported to slam shut. People have also smelled fresh apple pie.

THE MARSHALL HOUSE HOTEL

As one of the oldest hotels in the oldest city, few hotels if any in Savannah can compare to the charm and historic authenticity of the Marshall Hotel. The Marshall House was built by Mary Marshall in 1851.

During the railroad boom of the 1840s and 1850s, Savannah was growing. The railroad was bringing new businesses to Savannah, and with new businesses come people. Mary Marshall was a businesswoman who developed several properties, most notably the Marshall House. Mary Marshall and her estate leased the Marshall House until 1914. Marshall was a prominent figure through much of Savannah's turbulent history. She was born during the last year of the Revolution and died at the age of ninety-three in 1877.

The history of Marshall House spans 168 years. It played a role during two yellow fever epidemics in the mid-1800s as a hospital. During the final months of the Civil War, the Marshall House was used as a Union hospital.

From 1895 to 1899, it was closed. In 1899, the Marshall House reopened as a hotel. It had electric lights and hot water on every floor. In 1933, Herbert W. Gilbert, a hotel and real estate man, leased the building and changed the name to the Gilbert Hotel. It operated on and off as a hotel until 1957, when it closed again. The second, third and fourth floors were abandoned. The first floor was used by various shopkeepers and stores until 1998. In 1998, renovations began. It was extensively restored and reopened in 1999.

The Marshall House has received numerous awards over the years. It received awards from the Georgia Trust for Historic Preservation and the Historic Savannah Foundation. It is the recipient of multiple Best of Savannah awards. It also received TripAdvisor Certificates of Excellence. It has been featured on the Travel Channel's *Great Hotels*, *Good Morning America*, Fox News and the Travel Channel's *Haunted Hotel* program.

A portrait of Mary Marshall painted by Peter Laurens in 1830 hangs behind the front desk. Mary's husband's portrait hangs above the fireplace in the library. The Marshall House is known as one of the most haunted places in the entire state.

It's rumored that during the Civil War, when the Marshall House was used as a Union hospital, doctors had to bury the amputated arms and legs under the floorboards. It was an extremely cold year, and the ground froze solid. Rumor has it that during the 1998–99 restoration, construction workers were replacing the floorboards and found human remains. (I could not find anything to confirm that human remains were found.)

Some of the ghostly activity that has been seen and heard around the Marshall House includes a Union soldier with only one arm walking through the lobby. Stretchers with bodies on them have been seen being carried in the basement. Sometimes amputated limbs have been seen scattered on the basement floor. Men in Civil War uniforms wandering around the halls have been reported by hotel staff.

Guests have reported waking up at night with one of their arms outstretched as if a nurse was trying to find a pulse, while others have reported the unnerving feeling of being touched while in bed. Faucets have turned on spontaneously, and doorknobs rattle when no one is there. Children have been seen and heard playing and running in the hallways. Lights flicker on and off; electronic items turn themselves on and off, toilets overflow for no reason and disembodied voices have been heard. The sounds of heavy objects falling on the fourth floor have been heard. When someone goes to check it out, there's nothing there.

There are rumors of a ghostly cat being seen. The spirit of Mary Marshall has been seen in the hallway. Guests have reported hearing the sound of an old-fashioned typewriter coming from the room of author Joel Chandler Harris, who is famous for writing the Uncle Remus stories. Other guests have reported seeing a gentleman reading a book by the window. A lady in white has been seen in the hallways, and the sounds of babies crying have regularly been reported by some guests.

One boy reported being bitten on the arm by a boy he was playing with in the bathroom. When his mother looked in the bathroom for the other boy, no one was there. The boy had a bite mark on his arm. There have been reports of other guests being bitten somewhere on their bodies. Some guests have reported an awful odor that smelled like rotten flesh.

In the old operating room, people have reported seeing doctors treating soldiers. A female guest was staying at the hotel and reported seeing a shadow in her room of a man dressed like a Civil War soldier with a small boy. The guest said the man shouted at her, "Get out of my room." She grabbed her suitcase and made a strategic withdrawal. Some people have reported that they had an eerie feeling. Some people have heard the sound of marbles being rolled on the floor, and some have heard a rubber ball bouncing in the hallway.

Here is a list of haunted honors that the Marshall House has received listed from the Marshall House website www.marshallhouse.com:

- Number one of "11 of the south's most haunted places" by *Southern Living*, August 2016
- The Marshall House was featured in Visit Savannah Blog, "six most haunted places in Savannah you can visit," May 2016
- Named the eighth most haunted hotel in the world by *USA Today*, October 2015
- Named the most haunted hotel in Georgia by Yahoo October 2015.
- Featured on the *Today Show*, October 2015
- *USA Today*'s "10 best," named one of the most haunted hotels in the United States, October 2015
- *South Magazine* feature "Sleeping with the Spirits," April 2015
- Featured in *Huff Post* article "6 Hotels with Super Disturbing Pasts," April 2015
- Named "10 Best: Most Haunted Spots in the USA," *USA Today*, October 2014
- Named "10 Most Haunted Spots in USA," by 11 Alive Atlanta, October 2014
- "Haunted Hotels Provide the Perfect October Getaway," FoxNews.com, October 2011
- The Marshal House was selected as no. 5 in a *USA Today*'s 2015 10 Best Readers' Choice Travel Award contest for Best Haunted Hotel

THE BLEEDING HOUSE

Just before midnight on September 8, 1987, seventy-year-old Minnie Winston got out of the bathtub and noticed some red stuff on the bathroom floor. Minnie immediately woke up her seventy-nine-year-old husband, William. She asked William to come see all the red stuff on the bathroom floor. Spots of red stuff ranging in size from the size of a dime to a silver dollar were on the floor and lower walls. As they looked around the house, they found the red stuff in the bedroom, the kitchen, the basement, the halls and under the television. They had rented the house for the past twenty-two years at the corner of Fountain Drive and Morris Street in southwest Atlanta, and nothing like this had ever happened.

On closer inspection, they realized that it looked a lot like blood. Minnie called the local police department. When homicide detective Steve Cartwright arrived on the scene, he checked the house for a break-in. He couldn't find any evidence that a crime had been committed. His team went through the house for hours, making sure no one injured was hiding in the house. William and Minnie insisted that the blood did not belong to either of them.

Cartwright and his team collected samples of the blood and sent it to the state crime lab. Lab tests from the state crime lab confirmed it was type O human blood. Larry Howard, the state crime lab director, said it could be a homicide or it could be a hoax. The police were not calling it either. Minnie and William both had different types of blood. With the amount of blood they found that night, Detective Cartwright was sure about two things: it was human blood, and it did not come from the Winstons. Whose blood was it, and how did it get all over the Winstons' house?

When the media picked up the story, calls started coming into the Winstons and the police department from as far away as California. Calls were coming in from newspapers and TV and radio stations from across the country. The Winstons and the police station were flooded with calls. The Winstons found themselves besieged with curious spectators.

The Homicide Bureau and the State Crime Lab never identified the source of the blood, nor did they detect any indication of it being a hoax or a crime. Minnie and William Winston never experienced any further incidents with the blood. The police had to drop the investigation for a lack of evidence that a crime had been committed.

GILMER COUNTY BIGFOOT

One day in May 2019 as he was headed home, fifty-one-year-old E. Lee reported seeing a seven-to-eight-foot-tall dark-colored hairy creature with a pointed head that walked on two feet like a human with long arms swinging back and forth. Lee's sighting happened at around 8:30 p.m. It was still light. Lee pulled over on the side of the road and stopped when he saw the creature. He stopped by a small patch of woods hoping the creature would come out on the other side, but it never did. The creature was walking along a mountain highway, State Highway 515, in Cherry Log. Cherry Log is between the towns of Ellijay and Blue Ridge.

Lee told the *Charlotte Observer* that he feared being ridiculed like so many others have over the incident. Lee believed that he saw a Bigfoot while on the way home. The story led to talk about a legendary Bigfoot being on the loose in the Rich Mountain wilderness area.

A Bigfoot is an ape-like creature that cryptozoologists believe roams the backwoods of America. Conclusive evidence of the existence of Bigfoot has never been found. *National Geographic* reports that there is a wealth of circumstantial evidence for the existence of Bigfoot such as reliable eyewitness accounts, blurry photographs and mysterious unidentifiable footprints. Bigfoot sightings occur in every state in the United States.

THE BELL HOUSE

Let's drop in on Valdosta and check out the Bell House. Located on Ashley Street near downtown Valdosta, the Bell House is the city's number-one haunted spot. The 145-year-old house with its grand exterior has some strange things going on inside its walls.

The Bell House has been a pizza place, a Cajun restaurant, a bed-and-breakfast and, of course, home to Dr. David S. Bell.

Dr. David S. Bell was a medical practitioner and a businessman known for creating a miracle cure-all elixir during the Great Depression. Just for the record, Bell was not a true medical doctor. Bell was a medicine man. He adapted the title of doctor as part of his persona. Bell was the owner of a traveling medicine show, and he would set up in farming communities to sell his elixirs. Bell had one remedy called "Re-Nue-U," which Bell said would bring you back when you're gone. Maybe Bell drank some of his own tonic. He was known to pay off some of the local constabulary so they would not look too close at his shows.

Bell was known to dabble in other ventures, such as the Rustic Patio, where the then-unknown Ella Fitzgerald performed in the 1930s. During World War II, Bell tried his hand in the real estate business but eventually returned to his miracle cures.

Bell developed a pyramid scheme to promote his "Re-Nue-U" tonic. So much money was pouring into Bell's operations that the FBI became interested. The FBI stationed an agent at the post office to watch the sorting of Bell's mail and shut down his pyramid business scam.

Dr. Bell's last known business was fortune-telling. He had an Arabian-themed room in his house where he would bring his customers. Bell dressed like a sheik and would tell people's fortunes with the help of a crystal ball.

After Bell's death at age seventy on January 6, 1964, strange things began to happen in his house. Robert Nixon saw an apparition of someone walking through the house when it was being used as a restaurant. The apparition walked through the dining room, around the bar and vanished. In 2004, Southern Ghost Hunters Paranormal Investigations of Georgia did an investigation in the home. They found residual activity in it while it was Vito's Pizzeria and Lounge, and EVPs were captured upstairs.

Countless visitors and employees have reported hearing strange sounds. Impressions have been seen on the beds as if someone was lying on them when no one was there. There have been sounds of dogs barking when there were no dogs around. Some employees have reported encounters that were later found to be an exact match to Dr. Bell. Employees and customers have reported chairs moving, lights coming on and off and experienced cold chills in some rooms.

Parapsychology professor Doctor William Roll from the State University of West Georgia and a group of his students did an investigation in the Bell House. One student reported feeling a presence pressing down on her. Another student reported smelling cigar smoke. A magnetometer, which measures magnetic fields, was used. Near the Magnolia Room, the meter read 185.3, which is astronomically high. High readings were also found in the Peach Room. Roll suspected that these readings were caused by the house's electric wiring.

Some believe that Doctor Bell still lives in his house in the spirit form. Could this be a testament that Dr. Bell's "Re-Nue-U" elixir really works?

JOHN WESLEY MONUMENT

John Wesley was born on June 28, 1703, in Epworth, Lincolnshire. After receiving his education, he worked as a priest and curate. At the invitation of James Oglethorpe, John Wesley sailed to Savannah along with his brother Charles. Charles would serve as Oglethorpe's secretary. Less than six months after his arrival, Charles sailed back to England.

John Wesley would serve as the minister to the new Parish of Savannah. Wesley was greatly impressed with a group of Moravians that he sailed with to the New World. On arrival in Savannah, Wesley began his ministry. After two years in Savannah, he sailed back to England.

Wesley was recognized more for his work in Britain. While in England, Wesley became one of the leaders in the founding of evangelical Methodism. Wesley gave thousands of sermons during his lifetime. He died on March 2, 1791, and was laid to rest at Wesley's Chapel in London, England.

In 1967, the United Methodist Church of Georgia commissioned the John Wesley Monument. It was sculpted by Georgia artist and Methodist Marshall Harrison Daugherty. The statue was cast at the Roman Bronze Works in Corona, New York. The monument is eighteen feet high—a nine-foot statue standing on a nine-foot base. The monument was set in place in Reynolds Square in July 1969 but wasn't dedicated until August 3. John Wesley is dressed in a clerical robe with a Bible in his hand. In 1976, Reynolds Square was designated a Methodist landmark.

The $60,000 cost was shared by the church and its members, with the remaining coming from Savannah residents and local historical organizations.

Yellow fever wasn't the only disease that plagued the people of Savannah in the early days. Malaria was another dreaded disease that affected the people. Legend says that there was a hospital with a crematorium near what is now Reynolds Square. The patients that died in the hospital were wrapped in sheets and their bodies burned in the middle of what's now

Reynolds Square. It is believed that some of the patients were not fully dead when they were cremated.

Visitors have reported when taking pictures of Wesley's monument that strange apparitions show up in some of the pictures. Strange colors and patterns are said to appear, and orbs also show up in some pictures taken around John Wesley's monument.

TRACK ROCK GAP PETROGLYPHS

Track Rock Gap is located in the Chattahoochee National Forest in Union County near Blairsville. Located there are six table-size soapstone rock boulders containing more than one hundred carvings or petroglyphs. These petroglyphs were probably created by the Creek and Cherokee Indians beginning more than 1,000 years ago. Another source says that some of them could have been carved as long ago as 3,600 years ago.

The National Forest Service works closely with the Creek and Cherokee tribal governments to manage and protect these sacred sites. Tucked away in the gap between Thunderstruck Mountain and Buzzard Roost Ridge is one of the most significant rock art sites in the southeastern United States. This is the only site located on public land in Georgia. In 2009 research was sponsored on the site by the Chattahoochee Oconee National Forest. The research program was headed by archaeologist Johannes Loubser.

The petroglyphs show a wide range of figures like animals, bird tracks, circles with crosses, human footprints and many other carvings. The Indians used one of two techniques to carve the petroglyphs, pecking or incising the images into the soapstone rock. Archaeologists believe the Indians began this more than one thousand years ago. What makes this rock art so unique is that there is a lot of mystery surrounding the area.

Track Rock Gap is open to the public, and no fee is charged. The best time to visit is early in the morning or late in the afternoon when the sun is at an angle.

HISTORICAL MARKER

Track Rock Gap is one of the most significant rock art sites in the southeastern United States. It consists of six table-size soapstone boulders containing hundreds of symbols and figures. The carvings were made by Native Americans beginning around CE 1000. While the exact origin of the carvings is uncertain, the Cherokee name for the gap is Datsu' Nalsagun' Yi, "Where There Are Tracks."

The carvings at Track Rock were created in one of two ways. Many of the figures were created by pecking. Hard rocks or hammer stones were used to create shapes by repeated blows in the same spot until the desired shape was created. Alternatively, some of the figures were created by incising or carving into the rock. A hard stone would be rubbed back and forth to create a design.

The carvings at Track Rock were likely made for several different reasons. Some of the carvings may have been made to symbolize an event that occurred or to influence a future event. Many of the figures represent spirit beings or the actions of spirits. Perhaps the best way to understand Track Rock is as a sacred place for the people who created their carvings. Hope you enjoy your visit, but please do not mark on, damage or destroy the fragile elements.

THE GHOSTS OF ANDERSONVILLE

Andersonville began as a stockade eighteen months before the end of the Civil War to hold Union prisoners captured by the Confederate army. The twenty-six-and-a-half-acre Camp Sumter, later renamed Andersonville, was located deep in Confederate territory. It was originally named after the county in which it was located, Sumter County.

It was designed to hold ten thousand Union prisoners at a time, but as the war progressed, it held more than thirty-two thousand prisoners. The conditions were horrific, with minimal shelter. Some of the soldiers arrived wounded and later died. Many of them were starving, and disease was rampant from contaminated drinking water and harsh weather conditions. Dehydration, malnutrition, physical abuse, insects, yellow fever, gastrointestinal complication, smallpox and scurvy were some of the diseases that took the lives of many soldiers. Due to the deteriorating economy, the Confederate government was unable to provide the prisoners with adequate housing, food, clothing or medical care.

In the prison's fourteen months of existence, about 45,000 prisoners came through the prison's door—12,920 died and were laid to their eternal rest in a cemetery created just outside of the prison.

On July 26, 1865, the cemetery was established as Andersonville National Cemetery. By 1868, there were 13,800 Union soldiers who had been brought there after their deaths in hospitals, battles or other prisoner-of-war camps throughout the area. Beginning in February 1864, the initial interments were trench burials. The cemetery has been in continuous use since it was established. Today, it currently averages 150 burials a year.

The cemetery and prison site became a unit of the National Park System in 1970. Now the Andersonville Historic Site has three parts: the former site of Camp Sumter Military Prison, Andersonville National Cemetery and the National Prisoner of War Museum. The museum opened in 1998 to honor all U.S. prisoners of war in all wars. Today, the cemetery has nearly twenty thousand interments.

Congress stated in authorizing legislation that the park's purpose is "to provide an understanding of the overall prisoner of war story of the Civil War, to interpret the roll of prisoner of war camps in history, to communicate the sacrifice of Americans who lost their lives in such camps and to preserve the monuments located within the site."

Andersonville started as a railroad town and was named after John Anderson. Anderson was one of the directors of the South Western Railroad in 1853. The town of Andersonville played a role in the Civil War. It served as a supply depot and also had a blacksmith shop, a general store, saloons, a schoolhouse, some houses, a church and a post office.

Many visitors say that they can hear the cries and agony of the Union soldiers as they breathed their last breaths. Phantom soldiers have been reported to appear and then vanish just as quickly as they appeared. Civil War reenactors have reported developing a strange sickness during the night while camping out in or near Andersonville. Some visitors have reported being pushed by someone when no one was there. Visitors reported hearing the sounds of screams, soldiers marching and the sounds of gunfire. They have also reported hearing soldiers' names called. Others reported seeing figures walking in the fog that mysteriously falls on the grounds. Some visitors have reported hearing someone whisper in their ears when no one is around.

The superintendent and captain of the prison camp, Henry Wirz, was tried and hanged for war crimes. The hanging didn't break his neck; his body jerked until he was choked to death. Some say he has been seen walking the prison stockade. Some say the ghost of Captain Henry Wirz and the ghosts of other Union soldiers have been seen walking along the road that leads to the old prison. One visitor reported talking to a ghost

Two men camped about one hundred feet from the cemetery gate and were awakened slightly after midnight by an unusually pungent odor. After awakening, they heard the sound of a crowd in the distance. They heard the sound of a man talking but could not understand what he was saying. Small spirals of mist were seen rising up from the ground. Afterward, the smell disappeared, and the sounds and mist faded away.

The ghost of a Catholic priest has been seen standing near a curve in the road on rainy days. This ghost is believed to be Father Peter Whelan, a Confederate chaplain. There have been sightings of the ghost of a man with one leg using a crude crutch but not walking on the ground. He floats several feet above the ground. Some have reported a fog settling over the field and a campfire with men moving around it. Batteries will go dead for no reason. This could be one of the most haunted places in Georgia.

ANIMAL MUTILATIONS

A nimal mutilations date back to the 1700s, maybe even earlier. The question is, why would someone or something spend decades—possibly even centuries—roaming the land to collect animal parts? Cattle mutilations are the most prominent cases today. There have been cases of horses, sheep and other animals killed and mutilated.

The animal parts removed are usually the internal organs, tongue, lower jaw, sex organs, navel, heart and anus. The animals are drained of blood. There is no sign of the animal bleeding when the parts were removed or blood on the ground. The cuts are cauterized around the edges as if it cut with a laser. The parts are removed with surgical precision.

Who or whatever is slaughtering the animals does so without leaving any footprints, tire tracks or any other identifying marks around the slaughtered animal. Other animals' tracks usually stop at around thirty feet away from the dead animal. Circular depressions have been found around several sites. Flattened circles in crops or grass have occasionally been found with the animal lying inside.

In a few cases, residual radiation has been found in the area along with unidentified tranquilizing chemicals found in the animals. Veterinarians and many other scientists have studied cases of animal mutilations and come up empty-handed.

The FBI, local and state law enforcement are puzzled by the nature of the removal of the parts, the number of animals and the locations. The states with the most animal mutilations are Colorado, Texas, Montana, New

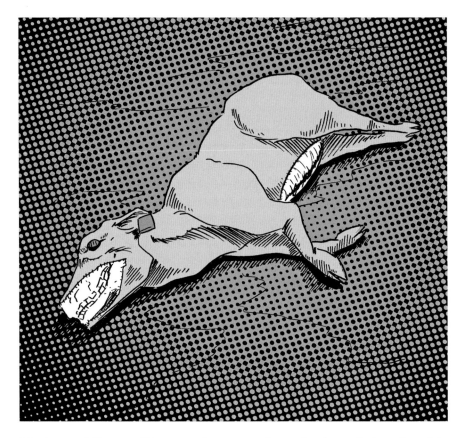

Mexico and Kansas. However, there are a few animal mutilations found in many other states.

Hall County was one of the sites of animal mutilations in Georgia. On their two-hundred-plus-acre farm in Flowery Branch, J. and K. Cooper lost more than twenty cows. The cows were found in wooded areas or gullies where it's harder to find them. In one case, a five-year-old pregnant cow was found dead and mutilated.

A report from the Hall County Sheriff's Office detailed the Coopers' yearlong nightmare with a mysterious predator that killed and mutilated over twenty cows on their farm in North Georgia from 2009 to 2010. No predator was ever seen, and no sign of anything around the dead animals was found. A report of a cow's death was made on October 18, 2009. The lower organs were removed. There were no holes in the animal consistent with a gunshot wound. There was a dark spot on the cow's neck. A few feet from the cow was another dark spot. Without having any tests run, the report said it looked like motor oil. The gates were locked, and there were no tire tracks leading from the gate. No one could have driven a motor vehicle to where the animal was.

On May 1, 2010, Cooper called the sheriff's office to report that he had found five of his cows killed and mutilated. These five cows were killed in the same area where several other cows had been killed. Apparently, Cooper didn't report all the cows that were killed.

Four days after the investigation was closed, Cooper called again; another cow had been found dead near the creek. Cooper took the cow's body to the University of Georgia for a necropsy. The results were never made available to the sheriff's office.

K. Cooper did several interviews with the media. She gave details that were not included in the sheriff's reports. She told the media that there was no blood anywhere. The udders and genitals were removed with surgical precision. No further law enforcement investigations were done.

Jackson County, Georgia, where two cows were found and mutilated, has law enforcement completely puzzled. There was no evidence of what caused their death. The only discernible evidence was that there was a clean cut around the rectal area. The first cows were found on December 16, 2009, said rancher Harold Edge. The University of Georgia determined that the cows were not diseased. When the second was found on January 6, Edge ruled out any kind of animal attack. There were no marks on the body or blood around the dead animal. The only mark on the cow was around the rear end.

In Walker County, several cows were killed and mutilated in the late hours of February 12, 2017. The Walker County Sheriff's Office was looking for an unidentified person or persons. The animals' deaths occurred in the area of Kingston Road and Highway 193 near the Walker County Fire Station Number Nine. There was no report found that said how the animals died or how they were mutilated.

There are a number of theories bouncing around about the cattle mutilations. These include, but are not limited to, predators, coyotes, vultures, rituals, devil worshipers and satanic cults. Black helicopters with no insignia or any identifying numbers and a large van-like truck with government plates have been seen around the area of some mutilations. The subject of secret government experiments has been brought up. Of course, there's the UFO theory, which is the most popular. Strange lights and unidentifiable crafts have been seen in the vicinity of many animal mutilations.

SPOOK BRIDGE

Every town has a ghost story or two that has been handed down from generation to generation. Haunted bridges are one that comes to mind. It seems that there's a bridge in at least every county where a murder occurred or an accident happened. The ghost of the person that died is still hanging around.

Lowndes and Brooks Counties seem to have a joining haunted bridge. The two counties meet along the Withlacoochie River. There the old abandoned spandrel arch bridge stands. The bridge is located on a closed section of Old Quitman Highway, aka Blue Springs Road, formally U.S. Route 84.

The locals simply call it Spook Bridge. The bridge was probably built in the late 1910s or early 1920s. The bridge has played host to a lot of fun times as well as tragedies. The land near the bridge was owned by the Walter Cunningham family. The Blue Springs Resort was located across the bridge at the train stop. The Blue Springs Resort attracted tourists from Georgia and neighboring states. There were cabins for the tourist to rent. There was also the Blue Hole, a natural spring, located in the tourist area.

In the mid-1940s, a gas truck ran into the bridge railings and tore down somewhere between fifty and one hundred feet. The railing was never repaired, leaving a dangerous area of the bridge.

Prior to 1970, two known drownings took place at Blue Hole. People would get drunk and dive off the tall cypress tree. If they hit the fifteen-foot hole they were ok, but if they missed the hole, they would land in about four feet of water.

In the 1940s, a flood washed out the roads around the bridge. In 1950, a new bridge was built in conjunction with Highway 84. The old bridge became abandoned.

In the early 1970s, everybody went down to the bridge. Around 1974 or 1975, graffiti started showing up; satanic signs and pentagrams were painted on the bridge. People started calling it Spook Bridge, and stories began circulating about ghosts and satanic rituals around the bridge.

A couple use to live in an old house on the Brooks County side of the bridge. Legend tells us that the man went crazy and killed his wife. Both of them haunt the bridge. Another version of the story is that the man and woman went walking on the bridge. The man pushed his wife off the bridge, drowning her. She haunts the bridge and can sometimes be seen trying to climb out of the water.

Another legend says that a boy and girl were driving across the bridge while courting. The car ran off the bridge, and they died in the river below. If you drive your car over the bridge, you can hear them pounding on the hood. There's another rumor that a busload of children ran off the side of the bridge.

A few years ago, a man was shot twice in the head execution style on the bridge. Richard A. Chafin, Brooks County sheriff, said they patrol the abandoned roadway and have made many arrests for trespassing.

RKDS Entertainment and Media filmed a movie called *Spook Bridge*. The movie features several actors and actresses from the Valdosta/South Georgia area. Most of the movie filmed in the summer of 2016 in Brooks County. Spook Bridge, of course, appears in the film. The movie spans from 1916 to the mid-twentieth century when the bridge was first built to the abandoned bridge of modern times.

PORTAL TO ANOTHER UNIVERSE

Many think that a portal to another universe is strictly science fiction or that another universe is equally science fiction. Maybe we just have closed minds. Maybe we should open our minds to new ideas. Who knows, maybe another universe does coexist with ours. If they do exist, and we discover them, then what are we opening the doors to?

In the last few years, there has been a lot more credibility given to the idea that there are possibly other dimensions and universes than ours. Scientists are exploring the idea that portals do exist. The theory is, if we can open a portal to another universe, would it be possible to travel through the portal to the other universe? On the other hand, could whatever occupies the other universe travel to ours?

Ever since the Large Hadron Collider—operated by the European Organization for Nuclear Research, or CERN—was put into operation in September 2008, there have been claims of interdimensional rifts. CERN operates the largest and most powerful particle accelerator in the world. The Large Hadron Collider is located three hundred feet underground, directly below the CERN control center in Geneva, Switzerland. The Large Hadron Collider is a loop reaching seventeen miles. This large loop is used to hurl subatomic particles at extreme speeds in order to smash them together to test what happens when they collide. CERN scientists are trying to unlock the secrets of our universe—they are also trying to re-create the conditions of the big bang (theory).

One of the most famous discoveries linked to the Large Hadron Collider was the observation of Higgs boson particles. Until this discovery, Higgs boson particles were purely theoretical.

There are those that fear that the Large Hadron Collider will create mini black holes or undo reality itself. There was an alleged ripple sent out from the facility in 2009 that was reported to have disrupted the earth's magnetic field and distorted space and time. Could such a thing happen? Could such a machine as the Large Hadron Collider destroy all mankind?

PURPORTEDLY, THERE IS A portal to another universe in Dublin, Georgia. It is located in the Monastery District and called Kcymaerxthaere. This alleged portal was created by a California geographer, Eames Demetrios. Demetrios has traveled the world over, placing markers at locations he believes exist in the literal world but also coexist in his lateral world.

Some believe the spot in the Gwome of Braethrens is a portal to an alternative universe. They have agreed to meet there if faced with impending disaster.

PLAQUE

Dublin's monastery district, once one of the larger in Kymaerica both in height and area, was all but destroyed in fighting with the Arrowhead Confederacy and their mobs of Geraldine mercenaries. Only this early example, the Monastery of the Fegren of the air, survived essentially intact, but ensnarled in severed cables that once were lines of life and friendship to other orders. As with most monasteries, a few floors below the rooftop farmscape was a ten foot thick, structure-wide plug of concrete protecting the brethren, their livestock, and their library—now swollen with salvaged and bloodied books—from hazards below

Discover Kymaerica
PLAQUE PLACED BY KYMAERICA.COM

CENTRAL STATE HOSPITAL

In 1837, Georgia lawmakers authorized the Central State Hospital for the lunatic, idiot and epileptic. When it opened in 1842, physicians were accepting all patients with misunderstood diseases. It was known as the Georgia State Lunatic, Idiot and Epileptic Asylum.

By 1872, the hospital had 112 patients per doctor. The doctors preferred using ropes and chains instead of programs designed to help rehabilitate the patients. Many of the patients housed in the asylum never left the facility alive, as evidenced by the twenty-five thousand graves across the two-thousand-acre hospital grounds. These were the unclaimed bodies. At its peak, it housed over thirteen thousand patients.

The Central State Hospital stands nearly abandoned today. Once consisting of nearly two hundred structures spread across the two thousand acres, it was one of the largest insane asylums in the United States. The remains stand as a testament to the many patients that were treated and mistreated.

By the 1950s, there were over twelve thousand patients, with one medical staffer per one hundred patients. Doctors used psychiatric tools of the time to treat the patients, such as lobotomies, insulin shock and electroshock therapy without any kind of sedation. Far less sophisticated techniques were also used. Children were confined to metal cages while many adults were forced to take hot steam and cold showers. Some were confined to straitjackets for weeks. Others were treated with douches or nauseants.

By the 1970s, Central State Hospital had begun to decline. Governors Carl Sanders and Jimmy Carter led the fight in transferring Central State's patients to other hospitals and clinics more suitable for patient care. In 2010, Central State Hospital officially closed its doors.

Four buildings were converted into prisons. Only one prison remains on the property today, along with the cook's building and the hospital for forensic patients. By the end of 2015, only nine buildings were occupied.

The Central State Hospital Local Redevelopment Authority, created in 2012, is trying to preserve the hospital campus. The grounds are closed to the public and protected by security guards. A tiny museum in an old railroad depot on the quad bears witness to the asylum's tumultuous past.

It's no wonder that the asylum is haunted. People have reported hearing strange voices. Strange sightings have occurred, and stranger occurrences have been reported. A sign placed on the property by the Georgia Historical Commission reads,

Georgia 1776

Milledgeville State Hospital

In 1837 largely through the influence of Tomlinson Fort and William A. White the legislature appropriated $20,000 for a dormitory near Milledgeville where the state's mentally ill could receive custodial care. A four-story building was opened on this site in 1842 and together with various later additions became known as the center building. Original serving only pauper patients, services were expanded for all bona fide citizens. Dr. Thomas M. Cooper (serving 1843–1846) was the first Superintendent and was followed by Dr. Thomas F. Green (1847–1879) and Dr. Theophilus O. Powell (1879–1907).

CRYBABY BRIDGE

Located in southern Harris County on Whitesville Road north of Columbus is a bridge that has earned the reputation of being a crybaby bridge. Like many other locations, the original bridge has long been torn down and replaced by a more modern one. It's the last of three bridges on an old dirt road. It is unclear if the incidents happened on the original bridge or the new one. I couldn't find a date when the old bridge was torn down.

Whether the incidents happened on the old bridge or the new, the haunting and stories still continue to this day. There are a number of stories and several variations surrounding the bridge. The stories have been passed around as urban legends for years.

The first story goes like this: a mother drowned her three children in the water below the bridge. They say if you park your car on the bridge on a night with a full moon and turn off the engine, it won't crank up for a few minutes. If you listen closely, you can hear the crying of the infant.

Another version of the story is that the children accidently drowned. People driving on the bridge on a night with a full moon have heard the distant sound of a baby and mother crying. Strange mists and fogs have been reported on the bridge. EVPs (electronic voice phenomenon) have supposedly been recorded on or near the bridge.

The second story is that of a baby that accidently drowned in the creek near the bridge; its spirit still haunts the area. The crying baby can be heard after dark around the bridge. Some say you have to be on the bridge to hear the baby crying.

The third story tells of a farmer that made a pact with the doctor that was to deliver his fifth baby. When the baby was born, the doctor would drown the baby in the creek without the mother's knowledge or consent. The father could not financially care for another child. The doctor took the baby as soon as it was born, walked down to the bridge and threw the baby to its death below. The baby and its mother have been seen in the woods near the bridge. Cold spots have been felt around the bridge. Footsteps have been heard coming toward people from the woods near the bridge. Some say that a figure dressed in white has been spotted floating through the woods near the bridge.

FOLEY HOUSE INN

The original owner of the Foley House Inn was a widow named Honoria Foley. She was married to Irish immigrant Owen Foley, and their house became the first bed-and-breakfast in Savannah, Georgia. Honoria Folly built the new home in 1896. Strangely enough, the second home was built over the ashes of the original house, which was destroyed by the great Savannah fire of 1889.

The Foley House Inn is a nineteen-room bed-and-breakfast located in the center of Savannah's historic district. The Foley House Inn's guests can enjoy luxurious accommodation along with a home-cooked to-order breakfast. Each room is uniquely decorated and comfortably furnished with a mix of antique furnishings. Many of the rooms have fireplaces, and some have a private balcony. All rooms have private baths. You can choose from luxury, premium, deluxe, garden level or carriage house rooms. The Foley House Inn also serves an afternoon tea and sweets from 3:00 to 5:00 p.m. In the evening, they serve wine and hors d'oeuvres. *Southern Living* magazine named the Foley House Inn the best inn in the South in 2017. Honoria Foley expired in 1917.

No inn would be complete without its resident ghost or ghosts. During renovations in 1987, workers tore down a wall and discovered that a skeleton had been walled up inside. Did they find a skeleton, or is this just a story? Could the person that the skeleton belonged to be the ghost?

One of the ghosts is believed to be the ghost of a gentleman that was trying to court Honoria Foley. The gentleman booked a room and kept

making passes at Honoria, but she would have no part of the gentleman. Legend says that one night the man sneaked into her room. Startled, Foley grabbed a candlestick and swung it with authority and sent the man to meet his maker. She killed him graveyard dead. The legend goes that Honoria was friends with a carpenter, and he helped her wall up the visitor.

Another story about the skeleton in the wall is that it was a wealthy boarder in the late 1800s who was murdered for his money. The staff has affectionately named the ghost Wally. Other ghost stories at the Foley House Inn include the man in a top hat seen walking through the garden. One guest reported that the man in the top hat pushed right by her going toward the front door and vanished through the door. He did not acknowledge that she was there. A little girl that screams out can be seen in the parlor. Another customer reported hearing footsteps on the staircase. She followed the footsteps to a random spot on the wall. While talking with the desk clerk the next morning, the desk clerk told her that was the place where the skeleton was found.

KENNESAW MOUNTAIN BATTLEFIELD

The Battle of Kennesaw Mountain was fought from June 19 to July 2, 1864. The Union forces were defeated, but the great loss of men did not stop General Sherman's march to Atlanta. Thousands of Confederate and Union soldiers lost their lives on the battlefield near Kennesaw, Georgia. More than 67,000 soldiers from both sides were killed, wounded or captured during the battle. General Sherman's Union army consisted of 100,000 men, 254 guns and 35,000 horses. General Johnston's Confederate army consisted of 63,000 men and 187 guns.

The 2,965-acre Kennesaw Mountain Battlefield is now a national battlefield to preserve the Civil War battleground of the Atlanta Campaign. Kennesaw Mountain National Battlefield Park was authorized for protection by the War Department in 1917. In 1933, it was made a unit of the National Park System. The name Kennesaw is derived from the Cherokee Indian word Gah-nee-sah, meaning "cemetery or burial ground."

Many people lost their lives during the war as it raged in the state of Georgia, leaving behind restless souls. In 2005, the park was named one of the Civil War Preservation Trust's ten most endangered battlefields due to the impact of urban growth and traffic congestion.

There have been reports of ghostly soldiers seen wandering throughout the battlefield. The sounds of cannon fire and gunshots have often been heard. The smell of gunpowder and blood has been described by witnesses. Cold spots have often been felt along the hiking trails.

Locals have reported encounters with Civil War soldiers who've just stopped by for a visit. The ghostly soldiers just seem to come and go for no specific reason through certain residential homes in the nearby neighborhoods.

On October 8, 2007, a man and his son were driving down one of the roads that goes through the Kennesaw Mountain Battlefield at night when out of nowhere a man on horseback appeared and ran across the road in front of them. They said it appeared to be a Union cavalry officer with a saber in his hand. The rider headed straight across the road and through a fence as if it didn't exist and vanished. Another version of the story has a car meeting them and the horseman going between the cars.

Some have reported feeling an eerie energy and seeing smoke as if it was coming from cannons.

A person with physical disabilities said that he was lying in bed and noticed the hazy form of what appeared to be someone in a Civil War uniform sitting on a horse standing in his bedroom. It vanished after a few seconds.

A lady was going around the corner of her house while taking out the trash when she came face to face with a figure dressed in an old-fashioned uniform. The lady dropped the trash and made a strategic withdrawal back into the house.

On June 24, 2000, a small group of young and old retraced their ancestors' steps on the Kennesaw Battlefield. They heard voices and saw dark shapes in the distance. As they moved on, footsteps could be heard up ahead of them on the path. Another one of the group said he saw a Union soldier in a ragged uniform with his left arm torn up walk by, look at him and then walk off into the woods. The same person said he looked at a trench and saw the heads of four soldiers watching them. At the camp, things got deathly quiet—not a night sound could be heard. They also encountered the overwhelming smell of something dead.

CHUNKS OF ICE FALLING FROM THE SKY

On October 27, 1959, a forty-pound chunk of ice fell out of the sky, crashing into a flower garden in Stephens County, Georgia. The chunk of ice left a hole in the flower garden as big as a car tire. The chunk of ice was pure water, and scientists concluded that it did not come from an airplane. There was no air traffic in the area at the time.

On October 29, 1959, a fifty-pound chunk of ice fell in Franklin County, Georgia. It was pure ice. There were no planes in the area at the time.

On October 3, 1960, a chunk of ice fell in Claude J. LeCroy's backyard in the town of Martin, which is located in Stephens and Franklin Counties. There were three witnesses to this ice event.

On a cold Saturday morning in January 2003, the bedroom of a young lady, her half sister and their pet dog might have been occupied, but the two girls had stayed elsewhere the night before. The home was in Lawrenceville in Gwinnett County, Georgia. At ten o'clock that morning, a basketball-sized chunk of ice crashed through their roof and hit the dog's bed in their bedroom. The dog was not in his bed at the time. The chunk of ice broke into several three-to-four-pound pieces. This incident made the news.

Federal Aviation Administration spokesman Christopher White reported that these cases are very rare. The Federal Aviation Administration did an investigation to see if it was caused by a passing plane, but the agency's findings were inconclusive.

Scientists investigating this type of thing say that ice falls of this size are extremely rare. The few that do happen are attributed to airplanes or

giant hailstones. Scientists have reported that in recent years space burgs are regularly entering the earth's atmosphere. They assume it's debris from comets. There is no way to tell how far space burgs have traveled through space before entering the earth's atmosphere and crashing to earth.

THE 1946 WINECOFF HOTEL FIRE

In the wee hours of the morning of December 7, 1946, the deadliest hotel fire in the history of the United States occurred. To this day, the Winecoff Hotel fire is still the deadliest hotel fire in the history of the United States. Located at 176 Peachtree Street in Atlanta Georgia, it was the tallest building in Atlanta, standing fifteen stories high. The Winecoff opened in 1913 and was advertised as 100 percent fireproof. It was named for the builder and owner, William Fleming Winecoff.

The third floor of the Winecoff caught fire at 3:30 a.m., and there was only one stairway in the whole hotel. There were no fire alarms, sprinklers or fire escapes. The fire's point of origin was the third-floor west hallway. A mattress and a chair had been placed in the hallway near the stairs to the fourth floor. It appeared the fire started there. The fire was first noticed by a bellboy responding to a guest's service call at 3:10 a.m. When he tried to leave the guest's room five minutes later, he noticed the hall was full of smoke.

The fire department was notified at 3:42 a.m. The first engine and ladder company arrived in minutes, but the ladders were not long enough to reach the upper floors. The firefighters were hampered, and some were injured by falling bodies. There were 385 firefighters, 22 engines, 11 ladder trucks and mutual aid from surrounding departments, which brought in 49 more pieces of equipment.

There were 280 guests in the hotel at the time of the fire. Many of the hotel guests died in their sleep and were burned too badly to be identified. Other guests chose to throw themselves out of the building and to their deaths.

Others died while trying to escape the building using makeshift ropes made out of bedsheets. In all, 119 lives were lost on the morning of December 7, 1946—30 of the those were part of a youth assembly scheduled to visit the Georgia State Capitol. The owner also perished in the fire.

Arnold Hardy, a graduate student at Georgia Tech, won the Pulitzer Prize for a picture he took of a woman in midair who had jumped from the eleventh floor and miraculously survived.

The Ellis Hotel, built on the same spot as the Winecoff Hotel, opened September 28, 2007. Employees in the Ellis Hotel have reported seeing ghosts moving around the hotel. Some employees have reported their tools missing. For two weeks straight, the fire alarm went off at 2:48 a.m. every night.

Georgia Historic Marker
THE WINECOFF FIRE
This is the site of the worst hotel fire in U.S. history. In the predawn hours of December 7, 1946, The Winecoff Hotel fire killed 119 people. The 15 story building still stands adjacent to this marker. At the time this building had neither fire escapes, fire doors nor sprinklers. For two and a half hours Atlanta fire fighters and others from nearby towns battled valiantly in the cold to save the majority of the 280 guests but their ladders reached only to the eighth floor and their nets were not strong enough to withstand jumps of more than 70 feet. Therefore numerous guests died on the sidewalks and in the alley behind the building. Thirty of the 119 victims were among Georgia's most promising high school students who had come to Atlanta to attend the YMCA's Youth assembly at the capitol. The Winecoff fire became the watershed event in fire safety. Within days cities across America began enacting more stringent safety ordinances. The fact that the Winecoff fire remains the worst hotel fire in U.S. history is testimony to its impact on modern fire safety codes.
This marker is dedicated to the victims, the
Survivors, and the firemen who fought the
Winecoff fire.
Georgia Historic Marker

SPONTANEOUS HUMAN COMBUSTION

On November 12, 1974, a sixty-six-year-old man named Jack Angel spontaneously combusted and lived to tell the tale of the hellfire. Angel spent a good amount of his life on the road working as a traveling salesman; he traveled throughout the United States selling his wares.

One evening while in Savannah, Angel finished his sales for the day, parked his motor home and settled in for the night. Angel fell asleep on the couch in his motor home. He awoke four days later with burn marks on his body but was in no pain. He had severe burns on his arms and body. His right hand was burned from the wrist to the fingertips. He also had a big hole burned in his chest. He also had burns on his legs, ankles and back.

Angel walked over to a hotel and collapsed. He woke up in the hospital, burned beyond belief. His hand was so badly burned that it become infected and had to be removed at the elbow. The doctor who examined him confirmed Angel was burned not externally but from the inside out. The doctor found quite a few nerves in his body that had been destroyed by the fire. Angel miraculously survived his ordeal.

No signs of fire were found in the motor home, and his clothes were not burnt.

We are all familiar with spontaneous human combustion. People simply burst into flames for no apparent reason. There is no scientific

explanation for this. The fire is so hot that the victim becomes nothing more than ashes. The fire never spreads to the surrounding area. Spontaneous human combustion cases can be found throughout history. Records go back to the 1600s.

FORT MOUNTAIN

Fort Mountain is part of the Cohutta Mountains, a small mountain range at the southern end of the Appalachian Mountains 2,850 feet above sea level.

Fort Mountain got its name from the remnants of a stone formation located on its peak. The man-made stone wall is 855 feet long. Nobody knows who or why the wall was built. It's commonly called "The Ancient Wall." It is 12 feet thick and up to 7 feet high and was built from stones from the local area. Some believe that it was built around CE 400–500. Others say that the date can't be determined.

There are some who believe it was built by the Spanish conquistador Hernando de Soto for protection from the Cherokee or Creek Indians around 1540. Another theory is that the wall was built by Madoc, the Welsh explorer who came to America in 1170. Some think it was built the moon-eyed people from Cherokee mythology.

Many generations of explorers, archaeologists, geologists and historians have wondered about the builders and the purpose of the wall. Some believe it was built for ceremonial purposes while others believe it was built for defense purposes. The true purpose of the wall and who built it remains a mystery to this day.

The historic stone tower in Fort Mountain State Park was built by the Civilian Conservation Corps in the 1930s as a fire lookout tower. It stood in ruins for more than forty years after being damaged by fire in the 1970s. The tower has been completely restored.

There is one legend that says a group of young men visited the historic site, and one of the young men asked his friend to take a picture of him. When his friend was taking the picture, he screamed and fainted. He was taken to the hospital and died two days later. The attending doctor said he died from a heart attack. When the picture was developed, there was a ghostly woman standing beside the young man. No one with him saw the woman when the picture was taken.

There are legends of people hearing the sounds of distant drums and seeing flickering lights and the ghostly images of men wearing bear skins.

SONIC BOOMS OVER GEORGIA

Seneca guns, sonic booms, sky quakes, exploding meteors, frost quakes, illegal fireworks, abrupt changes in the atmospheric temperature, top-secret government aircraft or UFOs and—here's a good one—climate change. It seems that climate change is getting blamed for everything these days.

Whatever the cause, loud booms have been heard across Georgia in the past few years. The U.S. Air Force and Navy made a joint statement that none of their planes was responsible for the loud booms. Both say they have no information on the booms.

These loud booms have been heard as far back as the 1800s off the shore of Lake Seneca in New York. That is where the term *Seneca guns* originated.

On August 4, 2019, several loud booms were heard near Marietta and West Cobb County. They occurred about five minutes apart and were very distinct.

On December 14, 2018, at 10:30 a.m. a loud boom was heard over Columbus County. The boom was so loud that it rattled windows and shook houses in Midtown Columbus County. The boom was heard as far away as Lake Harding. Officials from Robins Air Force Base said it was not the air force. An official at Fort Benning said it did not come from the army base.

In February 2016, loud booms that shook houses were reported in Banks County. The booms were so wide-spread that the Banks County Sheriff's Office could not pinpoint the sources.

On March 15, 2012, Southeast Georgia residents were shaken up by a series of loud booms between 8:15 and 8:30 a.m. The booms were heard in

Brantley, Camden, Charlton, Glynn and McIntosh Counties. They were so loud that buildings and windows shook. There were no earthquakes or any type of seismic activity reported by the U.S. Geological Survey. There were no reports of activity from the Naval Submarine Base Kings Bay, the navy or the army. The Federal Aviation Administration did not have any reports of aircraft going at supersonic speeds. Those booms are still unexplained.

Residents of Carroll, Douglas and Haralson Counties had their quiet time disturbed one Friday night by a loud boom at 9:45 p.m. The boom was so loud that it rattled windows across West Georgia. As of November 27, 2010, the National Weather Service in Peachtree City had no natural explanation. There were no military flights in the area.

No date was given for this boom. It happened about 5:30 in the evening over Chatham County. No one could say what direction the boom came from. WTOC TV 11 contacted the Chatham County Police and the Chatham County Fire department, but neither agency had any information on the booms. It was so loud that it was heard over Elba Island, Wilmington Island, Oatland Island, Talahi Island and Savannah's east side. No explanation has come from any local or government agency yet.

In 1884, two men heard booming sounds that appeared to come from underground in the mountains at Rabun Bald. The sounds continued until the wee hours of the morning.

On June 24, 1981, a booming sound occurred that shook houses in coastal Georgia and North and South Carolina. There was no air traffic in the area or seismic disturbances. Scientists theorized that a chunk of the continental shelf had mysteriously broken off and fell into the Atlantic Ocean. That would have caused a seismic disturbance at least.

On January 7, 1987, sometime during the night, three separate booms shook Central Georgia. One of the booms, which lasted about ten seconds, was picked up by a seismograph operator at Eatonton Georgia Tech. Seismologist Dr. Tim Long was on duty and monitoring the seismograph when the boom occurred. It's possibly an atmospheric occurrence of some type, but Dr. Long said the source could not be identified.

SAVANNAH THEATER

On December 4, 1818, the Savannah Theater opened its doors for the first time. The shows presented were the *Soldier's Daughter* and *Raising the Wind*. The Savannah Theater is the oldest continuously operating theater in the United States. This historic theater is located at 222 Bull Street on Chippewa Square. The theater's designer and architect, William Jay, was born in 1792 or 1793. The interior of the theater was decorated by Englishman William Etty, and it changed owners several times over the years.

The appearances of major performers marked significant moments in the history of the Savannah Theater. Many famous people have graced the stage of the Savannah Theater, including Fanny Davenport, W.C. Fields, Edwin Booth, E.H. Sothern, Julia Marlow, Otis Skinner, Henry Irving, Sarah Bernhardt, Tyrone Power, Ellen Terry, Lillian Russell, Ty Cobb and Oscar Wilde, just to name a few.

The theater is housed in a three-story building that features outstanding beauty along with its spectacular sign. The theater survived the hurricane of 1898. The hurricane tore off sections of the roof and flooded the auditorium. The theater caught fire in 1906 and then again in 1948 and survived both of those.

In a news article from 1895, the owner said when he went to open the theater he found a hole burnt in the floor of one of the dressing rooms. The fire must have put itself out because nothing else was burned. He reported that several policemen reported hearing strange noises inside the theater late at night only to find nothing there when they investigated it.

A group of lady dancers were changing costumes when they felt the sensation of being watched. No one was in the room but the dancers. The feeling got so strong that the dancers left the dressing room in different stages of undress.

Some believe the Savannah Theater is cursed. The source of the curse just might be a penny. When the theater was being renovated, an old 1818 penny was found inside one of the brick walls. The owner of the theater, Fred Weis, took the penny and carried it with him at all times. One day in 1948, Weis took a trip to New York, where he lost the penny. After he lost the penny, the theater caught fire and suffered severe damage.

This story doesn't have a date. Long ago, a boy named Ben was playing in the area near the spotlight, and for some unknown reason Ben died. From time to time, the spotlight operators would feel someone pull at the back of their shirt. When they turned around to see who it was, no one was there. They assume it's Ben still playing in the area.

In 2007, a girl on a ghost tour was sitting in one of the theater seats, and her closest neighbor was several rows back. She had a feeling that someone was behind her. She kept looking back but could see only the person a few rows back. No one was immediately behind her. All the seats were empty.

The tour guide later told her that he saw shadows in the area where she was sitting.

Another story involves actors seeing a ring of fire form in one of the dressing rooms only to put itself out just as quickly as it started. There were never any signs of a fire.

Some of the staff have reported that they have seen shadowy figures just appear and then disappear. They have also reported hearing performances on stage long after the show has ended and all the actors have left the stage. When they went to check it out, there was no one there.

GEORGIA GUIDESTONES

One of the most mysterious and intriguing granite monoliths ever built in the United States stands in an open field in Elbert County near the South Carolina border. The Georgia Guidestones, also known as the American Stonehenge, are located seven miles north of Elberton, Georgia, on Highway 77.

The stones are made from local granite. On a Friday afternoon in June 1979, a mysterious stranger calling himself R.C. Christian walked into the office of Elberton Granite Finishing Company and spoke to the president of the company, Joe H. Fendley Sr. Fendley was shocked when Christian explained what he wanted. No one knows who paid for the granite structure. Some believe the Rosicrucian Order financed the project. It is said that some of the workers complained about hearing strange noises and feeling dizzy while working at the site. The finished monolithic structure weighed 119 tons. The stones were unveiled on March 22, 1980. The Georgia Guidestones sit on the highest point in Elbert County, said to be sitting on an energy vortex.

The nineteen-foot-high monument displays a ten-part message on five massive slabs of polished granite situated in a star pattern, with four of them weighing more than twenty tons each. Together they support a twenty-five-thousand-pound capstone that is astronomically aligned with the summer and winter solstices. The Guidestones serve as a celestial clock, astronomical calendar and compass. Every day at noon, the sun shines

through a narrow hole in the structure and illuminates the day's date on an engraving. The Guidestones are positioned in an X pattern. Each line of the axis is oriented toward specific areas of the moon's annual rotation around the earth.

The Guidestones contain a written message to all of mankind and to future generations in twelve different languages. The names of four ancient languages are sandblasted on the sides near the top. They are Babylonian cuneiform, classical Greek, Sanskrit and Egyptian hieroglyphics.

There is a basic message along the square capstone: "Let these be Guidestones to an age of reason." The other languages represented on the Guidestones are Arabic, Chinese, English, Hebrew, Hindi, Russian, Spanish and Swahili.

There's an eye-level oblique hole drilled into the Gnomen stone facing upward toward the heavens and situated where the viewer can locate the North Star, Polaris. In the middle of the Gnomen stone is a large slot with a hole cut in it orienting the movement with the summer and winter solstices.

A message carved into the Guidestones gives a direct and specific mission to apocalypse survivors. The Guidestones are built to survive the apocalypse.

A tablet in front of the monument reads, "Let these be Guidestones to an age of reason." There are rumors that a time capsule is buried under it.

The Guidestones were vandalized in 2008. They were spray painted with the message, "Death to the new World Order. The Guidestones have ten mandates on them, offered to ensure humanity's future survival.

1. Maintain humanity under 500,000,000 in perpetual balance with nature.
2. Guide reproduction wisely—improving fitness and diversity.
3. Unite humanity with a living new language.
4. Rule passion, faith, tradition, and all things with tempered reason.
5. Protect people and nations with fair laws and just courts.
6. Let all nations rule internally resolving external disputes in a world court.
7. Avoid petty laws and useless officials.
8. Balance personal rights with social duties.
9. Prize truth, beauty, love, seeking harmony with the infinite.
10. Be not a cancer on the earth, leave room for nature, leave room for nature.

COLONIAL PARK CEMETERY

Colonial Park Cemetery was established around 1750 as the original burial ground for the Christ Church Parish. In 1789, the cemetery was enlarged to be used by all people no matter what denomination.

More than 700 who perished during the yellow fever epidemic of 1820 are buried there. The cemetery was closed to burials in 1893. During the height of its use as a cemetery, there were over 10,000 people buried there. There are fewer than 1,000 graves with markers left. Some stories say that the exact number of yellow fever deaths were 666.

During the Civil War, Federal troops took over the cemetery grounds when they occupied Savannah. There were many graves looted and desecrated by the troops.

Many of the graves are resting under modern-day Savannah. Bodies have been discovered quite frequently during the city's expansion. Colonial Park Cemetery is in the middle of Savannah's Historic District, located on the corner of Abercorn and Oglethorpe Streets. The oldest extant cemetery in Savannah has served as a park since 1896, when the city took over the cemetery from Christ Church.

No cemetery would be complete without its resident ghosts. The first story is that a maid at the Old City Hotel was found outside the cemetery gate with tears in her eyes. When her co-workers found her and asked what was wrong, she said that she had followed a young man from the hotel to the cemetery, when he just disappeared. (I couldn't find a reason why she followed the young man.)

Another story tied to the cemetery says that Rene Asche Rondolier was convicted of the murder of two young girls. Rondolier was hanged inside the cemetery for his alleged crimes. Many visitors say that they have seen a man hanging from a tree, while others say they saw a man walking around the cemetery. It would be hard to mistake Rondolier because he was extremely tall.

There are stories of shadowy figures moving around the cemetery. There's also a story about a green mist moving among the headstones. Young children dressed in period clothes are often seen around the cemetery. Some have reported a grim reaper figure that often appears on the southern side of the park. Visitors have reported seeing a floating couple.

The red-hued image of a young girl has supposedly been captured in photographs. She is often captured when she is kneeling at a grave. One boy stopped and talked to the ghostly girl. He asked her what she was doing in the cemetery. He said that the little girl asked him to remain.

The historical marker
In this cemetery many victims of the
Great Yellow Fever Epidemic
Of 1820 were buried.
Nearly 700 Savannahians died
that year, including two local
physicians who lost their lives
caring for the stricken.
Several epidemics followed. In 1854
The Savannah Benevolent Association
Was organized to aid the families
of the fever victims.

CALLAWAY PLANTATION

Callaway Plantation offers a glimpse into a bygone era. Once a working plantation, it started with a single log cabin built in 1785 by Job Callaway. By the 1860s, it had grown into a three-thousand-acre southern plantation with a brick mansion built by Aristride Callaway. The mansion was built with red bricks and tall white columns. When Aristride was thirty-four, he married a fifteen-year-old girl. They had nine children before she died at age forty-five. Callaway Plantation has passed down through four generations of Callaways, and the family cemetery is still on the plantation grounds. Callaway Plantation was given to the city of Washington, Georgia, by the remaining Callaway family.

Callaway Plantation is now a fifty-six-acre restoration project and is home to several unique historic structures. Still standing on the plantation is a 1785 log cabin, the Gray House from 1790, an 1840 Dally slave cabin, an 1891 one-room schoolhouse and a 1930 general store.

Picnic and RV facilities are on the site, with nine hookups available along with showers and restrooms.

One night, dogs started barking behind the big house. The caretaker and a friend went to see what the dogs were barking at. What they found startled the caretaker and his friend. There were four mounted riders in Confederate uniforms. As the riders, the caretaker and his friend stared at one another, the riders turned and rode off. The riders or horses didn't make a sound as they rode off in the direction of Washington and out of sight.

People have reported seeing shadows moving around a mirror on the second floor. The sounds of footsteps and voices have also been reported. Some have reported seeing the spirit of a child in the graveyard. Some have felt strange energies in different buildings.

INTERVIEW WITH LYNETTE GOODWIN

The year was 1992, and we were moving into an old plantation house in Twin City, Georgia. I was eleven years old, and my brother was twelve. We were excited about the move. It was a five bedroom, two and one-half baths with a porch that wrapped around the entire house. It was so beautiful. I got my own bedroom, which was across from the sitting room from my brother's. We weren't rich, but daddy always made sure we had a nice place to live.

My room was huge. It had six floor-to-ceiling windows and enough room to put two full-size bedroom suits in, which we did when my stepsisters came to visit. We had been living there for a couple of months, and my brother and I had settled in and it was starting to feel like home.

It was November 1992; we had just finished eating dinner, and I washed the dishes and cleaned the kitchen. I then decided to get my two-year-old niece, who was staying with us, and go to bed. As I was going through the door from the dining room into the sitting room, I saw a reflection in the window and it wasn't mine. There in the window was a man with dark hair holding my niece. It was strange because I remember I wasn't scared. I almost felt comfort. I looked down at my niece, who was sleeping in my arms. When I looked back, the reflection of the man was gone, and what was left was just the reflection of my niece and me. I just shrugged it off and went to bed. Later that night, I remember waking up feeling like I was being watched. Along with the feeling of being watched, I also felt comfort like I did earlier. When I sat up to look around the room, the same man I saw in the window was sitting on the extra bed just watching me. I know I should have been scared, but I wasn't. It was like he was just there watching over us.

I know he had to be a ghost or spirit because even though I could see him I could also see through him, almost like he was transparent. I never thought much more of it. All I know is we lived there for a year, and I always felt safe and at peace.

Another unexplained event took place one day when my brother and I came home from school to find our dad and stepmom in a frenzy. We asked what was wrong. Daddy said he wasn't sure. Daddy said they heard a little boy and girl playing in the attic. He heard them running around in the attic, giggling. He thought my brother and I might have skipped school so he went to the attic to get us—only no one was there. He said he even called the school to make sure we were there. Now my dad was a very serious man. He didn't believe in ghosts. He and my stepmom swore they heard kids playing in the attic, but no one was there. The next day, daddy contacted the homeowner, Mr. Perry Roundtree, and asked about the history of the house. Mr. Roundtree informed my daddy that it was an old plantation house and was 130 years old. It was used as a safe house for runaway slaves. Mr. Roundtree said that a husband and wife owned the house at that time and helped the slaves. Mr. Roundtree also said that the man and woman had two children, a son and a daughter.

When the safe house was discovered, the homeowners and both of their children and some runaway slaves were killed in the house.

It was weird thinking the man in my room and the kids daddy heard playing in the attic were probably the spirits of that same family. Mr. Perry Roundtree has passed on, but that beautiful plantation house still stands today.

Lynette Goodwin now lives in South Carolina.

ALBANY'S GHOST OF THE HEADLESS HORSE

This unique ghost story made headlines in newspapers across the country on July 9, 1888. This ghost story features an unusual ghost, the ghost of a big, white, headless horse.

It seems that a white headless horse haunts the banks of the Flint River in the vicinity of the fairgrounds in Albany, Georgia. More than one hundred years ago, the big attraction at the Albany riverfront was the ghost of a headless horse.

Dink Melvin, a local boatman and guide, said that he's seen it for the last five or six years. There was one time he thought it was trying to board his fishing boat. Melvin said if he gets in his boat and paddles across the river, the horse follows him to a certain place and then disappears.

There's no explanation why the ghost of a headless horse would haunt Flint River or why the horse is headless. It is one of Georgia's unique hauntings.

ONE FINAL THOUGHT

How do some people become an expert on ghosts? First of all, you can't prove or disprove the existence of ghosts. So how does one become an expert on something that can't be proven to exist? The same question goes for UFOs or Bigfoot.

All you have to go on is eyewitness accounts, which can't be verified unless there are a number of witnesses to the same happening. There are thousands, maybe millions of pictures and videos of these alleged things. All of these can be faked. Most of the pictures are blurred, out of focus, and you can't tell anything about them.

When you have a credible witness or multiple witnesses who see the same thing, then there is something there, but it still can't be proven. There are too many witnesses to the sightings for something not to exist. But what?

Why do people think that every shadow, cold spot, hot spot, flickering light or orb is a ghost?

Television has ruined the chances of being considered a serious hunter of the unexplained, such as ghosts, cryptids, UFOs or any other strange thing. Television is the biggest provider of faked pictures, videos and so-called experts. Television's sole purpose is to get people to watch their shows. So why not label someone as an expert and have them on hand to confirm it. The more people that watch television the more they can charge for commercials. Television is simply a money-making instrument. These shows tell people what they want to hear.

Let's stop calling everything supernatural or paranormal. It may not be either of those. Let's call it unexplained, since it's unexplained at the time. There may be a logical explanation for what is happening.

Is what we call a ghost a who or what? This has been a much-debated subject. When we see a ghost of a person, exactly what are we seeing? Is it the spirit of a dead person or an image from the past that you have to be at the right place at the right time to see it? Why do people think Halloween is a haunted day? What's so special about Halloween that all the ghosts want to come out? Why do people hunt ghosts at night? If it's haunted at night, then it's haunted in the daytime. When real evidence is finally discovered, no one will believe it.

REFERENCES

Letters

Herbert B. Loper, assistant to the Secretary of Defense (Atomic Energy), letter from Office of the Secretary Of Defense, June 9, 1958.

Books

Carmichael, Sherman. *Forgotten Tales of South Carolina*. Charleston, SC: The History Press, 2011.
———. *UFOs over South Carolina*. N.p.: Schiffer, 2014.
Coleman, Christopher K. *Dixie Spirits*. New York: Fall River Press, 2008.
Hauck, Dennis William. *Haunted Places*. New York: Penguin Books, 1996.
Holy Bible King James Version.
Marrs, Jim. *Alien Agenda*. New York: HarperCollins, 2000.
Miles, Jim. *Mysteries of Georgia's Military Bases*. N.p.: Schiffer, 2017.
———. *Weird Georgia*. New York: Sterling, 2006.
Newman, Rick. *Haunted Bridges*. Woodbury, MN: Llewellyn, 2016.
Roberts, Nancy. *Civil War Ghost Stories and Legends*. Columbia: University of South Carolina Press, 1994.
———. *Georgia Ghosts*. Winston-Salem, NC: John F. Blair, 2006.
Thay, Edrick. *Ghost Stories of the Old South*. Edmonton, AB: Ghost House Books, 2003.

Wangler, Chris. *Ghost Stories of Georgia*. Edmonton, AB: Lone Pine Publishing, 2006.

Historical Agencies

The Historical Marker Database

Law Enforcement

Walker County Sheriff's Office

Non-Government Agencies

Haunted History
National UFO Reporting Center

Newspapers

Associated Press
Atlanta Journal-Constitution
Brunswick News
Charlotte Observer
Daily Citizen-News
Henry Herald
Mariette Daily Journal
Newnan Times-Herald

New York Times
Oakland Tribune
Register Guard
Savannah Morning News
Times Enterprise
USA Today
Valdosta Daily Times

Magazines

Atlanta Magazine
Good Housekeeping
National Geographic
People Magazine

Skeptical Inquirer
Southern Living
Sportsman's Guide
Time Life

REFERENCES

Government Agencies

Georgia Department of Natural Resources, Wildlife Resources Division.
National Park Service.

Television

WBTV 3   CBS News
WTVC ABC 9   WTOC 11
Inside Edition

Newsletters

Filer's Files

Radio

Coast to Coast AM

Businesses

Page House Bed and Breakfast

Interviews

Lynette Goodwin

Websites

abcnews.go.com   astronomycafe.net
active.com   atlanta.curbed.com
ajc.com   atlantaplanit.wabe.org
aminoapps.com   atlasobscura.com
anomalien.com   battlefields.org

bellatravelplanning.com
beyondthecircle.net
blog.pinnaclecabinrental.com
brownsguides.com
cartercenter.org
cedarcreekcabinrentals.com
chattvoice.com
chronicles.roadtrippers.com
civilwarrailroadtunnel.com
clinchcountychamber.org
colorfulplaces.com
coyotestail.com
creativeloofing.com
crossingcreekrvresort.com
decktheholidays.blogspot.com
disclose.tv
earthsky.org
11alive.com
endtimesand2019.wordpress.com
en.wikipedia.org
exemplore.com
exploregeorgia.org
exploresouthernhistory.com
facebook.com
famoushotels.org
findagrave.com
foleyinn.com
forum.gon.com
foundationforparanormalresearch.org
fs.usda.gov
gafollowers.com
gaia.com
gardenandgun.com
gastateparks.org
gatewaymacon.org
gendisasters.com
georgia.gov
georgiacoast.com
georgiaencyclopedia.org

georgiahauntedhouses.com
georgiamysteries.blogspot.com
georgiaparanormalplaces.wordpress.com
georgiastatesignal.com
georgiatrust.org
ghostcitytours.com
ghostsandgravestones.com
ghosttheory.com
goldenisles.com
gosouthsavannah.com
hauntedgeorgia.wordpress.com
hauntedplaces.org
hauntedplacesofusa.blogspot.com
haunted-places-to-go.com
hauntedrooms.com
hauntedsavannahtours.com
hauntin.gs
history.com
historicghosts.net
historicwashingtonga.com
intothewonder.wordpress.com
jacksonville.com
jekyll-island-family-adventures.com
legendsofamerica.com
legendtrippersofamerica.blogspot.com
library.massasoit.edu
lighthousefriends.com
livescience.com
maps.roadtrippers.com
markgelbart.wordpress.com
marshallhouse.com
mentalfloss.com
metrospirit.com
monkeygirl176.tripod.com
movoto.com
mysteriousuniverse.org
mystery411.com
narcity.com
nationalforests.org

nationalparks.org
neatorama.com
newser.com
n-georgia.com
northfulton.com
npr.org
oaklandcemetery.com
okefenokee.com
oldgeorgiahomes.com
onlyinyourstate.com
ourgeorgiahistory.com
paranormalinvestigations.net
paranormalsoup.com
peopleofonefire.com
porterbriggs.com
realparanormalexperiences.com
reddit.com
reflectorgsu.com
revolvy.com
roadsideamerica.com
roadsidegeorgia.com
savannah.com
savannahga.gov
savannahterrors.com
scarestreet.com
scare-you-now.livejournal.com
seekghosts.blogspot.com
17thstreetinntybeeisland.wordpress.com
singularfortean.com
siprinvestagations.com
sjchs.org
skepticfiles.org
southernghosts.com
southernspiritguide.org

spoilertv.com
strangemag.com
theawl.com
thehauntedhighway.tripod.com
thehauntedlibrarian.com
the-inside-scoup.com
the-line-up.com
thenightsky.org
thescarechamber.com
theshadowlands.net
thevintagenews.com
thoughco.com
thoughtcatalog.com
thrillist.com
todayingeorgiahistory.org
28thga.org
247sports.com
tybeelighthouse.org
ufonewshub.com
ufoinsight.com
unexplainable.net
unexplainedmysteries.com
urbanlegendsonline.com
vacationsmadeeasy.com
visit-historic-savannah.com
visittybee.com
weather.com
werewolfpage.com
werewolves.com
wired.com
wrbl.com
yahoo.com

ABOUT THE AUTHOR

Sherman Carmichael, a native of Hemingway, South Carolina, currently lives in Johnsonville, South Carolina. Carmichael has been dabbling in things that are best left alone—like ghosts, UFOs, monsters and other strange and unusual things—since he was seventeen. He has seen, heard and felt things that defy explanation. Carmichael's first three books—*Forgotten Tales of South Carolina*, *Legends and Lore of South Carolina* and *Eerie South Carolina*—center on ghosts and the strange and unusual. In his fourth book, *UFOs over South Carolina*, Carmichael takes a closer look at hovering objects and strange lights in the sky. His fifth book, *Strange South Carolina*, returns to the ghostly encounters. In his sixth book, Carmichael takes a look at coastal North Carolina with *Mysterious Tales of Coastal North Carolina*. In Carmichael's seventh book, *Mysterious South Carolina*, the author returns to South Carolina. In his eighth book, *Mysterious Tales of the North Carolina Piedmont*, Carmichael takes a look at the mysterious side of the North Carolina Piedmont. Carmichael has traveled throughout the United States visiting haunted locations, including Roswell, New Mexico. He has also traveled to Mexico and Central America researching the Mayan ruins. He plans to continue visiting these unusual places for many years to come. Carmichael worked as a journalist for many years, thirty years as a photographer, thirty years in law enforcement and twelve years in the movie entertainment business.

HOW IT ALL BEGAN

It all began forty-eight years ago at the time of this writing (January 2020) with a copy of *Fate Magazine* and six boys with an inquiring mind. There was my younger brother Steve Carmichael, Mike Birchmore, Jason Birchmore, Earl Pope, Terry Owens and me. Steve Carmichael, Earl Pope and Jason Birchmore have long since gone home to meet their maker. As for Terry Owens, I lost contact with him many years ago. Mike and I still stay in contact.

We set out looking for anything with a strange story tied to it. With two cars between us and very little money, we didn't do a whole lot of traveling back then and not very far either. I always had a 126 or a 110 camera with me. I never got a picture of anything, and to this day I still haven't, not even with all the sophisticated cameras that I've used over the years. Years later, we had our first encounter with the strange and unknown. I can't remember who was with me or the year, but we were at Old Gunn Church, where we heard the faint sound of a church choir singing their favorite hymn. The story of Old Gunn Church can be found in my third book, *Eerie South Carolina* (The History Press, 2013).

In 2010, Skip Lyle productions and Jim Holcomb got me to research South Carolina legends for a proposed TV series. After filming the first episode, Skip Lyle closed the project. With a file cabinet full of research, I had to decide what to do with it. I could chunk it away or write a book. I wrote a book. I'm still writing and plan to continue.

How It All Began

I imagine I've annoyed countless librarians, newspaper reporters, paranormal investigators, museum staff, property owners, ghost tour guides, historical societies and others in my quest for stories about the strange and unknown. And it all started with six young boys and an interest in the unknown.